PLACES OF POWER

Measuring the Secret Energy
of Ancient Sites

Paul Devereux

BLANDFORD

KALAMAZOO PUBLIC LIBRARY

A Blandford Book
This edition first published in the UK 1999 by Blandford
A Cassell Imprint

Cassell plc
Wellington House
125 Strand
London WC2R 0BB

www.cassell.co.uk

First edition published by Blandford 1990

Text copyright © 1990 and 1999 Paul Devereux

The right of Paul Devereux to be identified as the author of
this work has been asserted by him under the provisions of the
UK Copyright, Designs and Patents Act 1988.

All rights reserved. No part of this book may be reproduced or
transmitted in any material form, including photocopying,
recording or storing it in any information storage and retrieval
system or by any electronic means, whether or not transiently
or incidentally to some other use, without application in
writing solely to the publisher and the granting of written
permission from the copyright holder and publisher except in
accordance with the provisions of the UK Copyright, Designs
and Patents Act 1988 or under the terms of a licence issued by
the UK Copyright Licensing Agency, 90 Tottenham Court
Road, London W1P 9HE.

Distributed in the United States by Sterling Publishing Co., Inc.,
387 Park Avenue South, New York, NY 10016-8810

A Cataloguing-in-Publication Data entry for this title is
available and may be obtained from the British Library.

ISBN 0-7137-2765-9

Typeset by Best-Set Typesetter Ltd
Printed and bound in Great Britain by
Biddles Ltd, Guildford and Kings Lynn

CONTENTS

INTRODUCTION TO THE
SECOND EDITION

Throughout the twentieth century, popular rumour has maintained that ancient sacred sites harbour strange powers. This belief has its origins in anecdotal reports of unusual happenings at such places, and centuries of folklore ascribing supernatural properties to old standing stones and mysterious earthworks. Numerous examples of such archaeo-gossip, traditional and modern, are given in the pages of this book. The Dragon Project was brought into existence in 1977 in order to see if there was any possibility that at least some of the rumoured magic was measurable. On a part-time basis, and with little funding, The Dragon Project could only make a start on this ambitious undertaking, but it did find evidence of noteworthy anomalies relating to background radioactivity and natural magnetism at certain monuments. Further to this, a stubborn body of anecdotal data presented itself concerning unusual light phenomena haunting the very locations favoured by the ancient builders of certain kinds of sacred monuments, and at places that had been deemed inherently sacred, such as holy hills and mountains. A scatter of other possible anomalous effects concerning infra-red radiation, ultrasound and other physical energies was also noted. The first edition of *Places of Power* was published in part to provide a summary of The Dragon Project's limited findings to date. The book also covered the fruits of additional research efforts undertaken by numerous other people, as well as by the present author. The book offered, and still does, the most comprehensive single-source account of what is objectively known about reported strange energies at places anciently considered as sacred.

Although little new objective work on this topic seems to have been carried out since the first edition of *Places of Power*, the opportunity arises here to note a few interesting developments.

RADIOACTIVITY

American researcher, Marsha Adams, has uncovered indications that a recurring symbol found in prehistoric Native American rock art in Arizona and Nevada may indicate locations of strong natural radioactivity. Adams has measured five sites where the rock art symbol in question appears. Increased amounts of radiation were found at four sites, while there were extremely strong radiation levels at one. Maximum radiation readings were found close to the symbol of interest. In at least one case, Adams had to undergo decontamination procedures when she returned home after fieldwork at the rock art sites. She feels that inferences to radiation can be found in some Native American ceremonial rituals and legends.

It is not proposed that ancient peoples went around with Geiger counters. However, it could be argued that human beings and other living organisms can sense the presence of unusual levels of natural radioactivity (see pages 186–99). In a currently unpublished work, 'Were Early Native Americans Aware of Naturally Occurring Radiation?', a version of which was presented as a paper at a conference of the Society for Scientific Exploration in the United States in 1997, Adams proposes that prolonged exposure to places with a certain type of radioactive material would likely result in certain physical conditions. Hypoxia could be indirectly produced due to the physical displacement of oxygen by a heavier gas, radon, that incidentally happens to be radioactive, and this in turn might produce fatigue, bouts of euphoria and other noticeable effects. She notes that other symptoms, such as lower fecundity, susceptibility to infection, mutation, and birth defects, could be generated by radiation directly. Ancient peoples would come to consider locations that engendered such conditions as being haunted by powerful, potentially dangerous, spirits.

On pages 199–202 it is noted that some people have experienced transient visionary episodes while at places with relatively high background radioactivity, and a condition we have nicknamed 'radiation-psi' is hypothesized. Since the original publication of *Places of Power*, Dean Radin, a leading parapsychological researcher who has made specific study of mental influences of background radiation (paper included in *Frontier Perspectives*, 1991), has confirmed that there is some evidence to support thinking along such lines. In 1996, Radin investigated Engsö Castle, a reputedly haunted Swedish site, and found higher radiation levels everywhere around and inside the castle than at any other site he and colleagues visited in Scandinavia.

LIGHTS AND SITES

References to unexplained light phenomena recur throughout this book. While these 'earth lights' have been specifically and culturally associated with certain temple sites and sacred spots around the world, the study of the phenomena themselves remains something of a neglected, fringe activity, too often mixed up with prejudices for and against UFOs. Nevertheless, new information continues to emerge. In *The Ley Hunter* (Issue 114, 1991) it was reported that observation of light phenomena issuing from the ground was used as a prospecting method by copper miners at the Bere Alston mine in Devon into the early twentieth century. In the science journal, *Nature* (6 December, 1990), Professor Marcel Ouellet of Quebec University announced that observers had made 52 sightings of light phenomena in the Saguenay-Lake St John region. The lights had been witnessed emerging from the ground and, in some cases, rising high into the air. Some of the lightballs were said to be between 3–5 m (10–16 ft) in diameter. They were seen between 1 November 1988 and 21 January 1989, and in the middle of this period there was an earthquake in the region.

In order to promote earth lights research, the present author worked on a major television documentary on earth lights, which was shown on Channel 4 (*Equinox*) in Britain, and on the Discovery Channel in North America. This involved field investigations in Australia and Mexico, and footage of light phenomena in various countries was shown. By a remarkable coincidence, a few hours after the British showing of the film in November 1996, strange lights started to be reported in Cornwall, the megalithic Mecca. These took the form of slow, lazy flashes of light in the sky, rectangles of light moving with 'precision', and moon-like luminescent globes which slowly dissolved. One week to the day after the broadcast, Cornwall experienced its strongest earthquake of the twentieth century.

MEGALITHIC MAGNETISM

Prompted by the accounts in the first edition of *Places of Power*, Philip Burton, a subscriber to *The Ley Hunter* journal, cast his liquid-filled magnetic compass around various sites that he visited. His findings were published in a series of reports called MAGCAT in *The Ley Hunter*. In his first selection (Issue 113, 1991), Burton found no unusual effect on his compass at the following sites in Gwynedd, Wales: Cae Maenllwyd standing stone (SH 43084444); Glasfryn standing stone (SH 40484231); Gwynus standing stone (SH34594203); Rhiw standing stone (SH 22602768); Tir-Gwyn standing stones (SH 34403921); Y Ffor cromlech (SH 39913489). These negative findings are important in that they show that magnetic stones are not commonplace at sites. While it could be argued that the existence of such magnetic sites is simply a function of the geology of the region in which they are situated, it is important to note that at another Gwynedd site (Bach Wen cromlech, SH 40764947), Burton found that the monument's north and south upright support stones deflected his compass needle. He also found a strong compass reaction on the large eastern stone at Mitchell's Fold, Shropshire (SO 305984), and at a stone in the circle's southwest quadrant (see also pages 118–20).

Magnetic anomalies at megalithic sites are facts, but whether they are meaningful facts is a matter of interpretation. The magnetic stones could simply be fortuitous, or they could have been deliberately employed as 'spirit stones' by the megalith builders. We may never know for sure, although it is likely that ancient peoples knew the subtleties of their geophysical surroundings, in the same way that we now know they knew their botanical environment (see in particular Chapter 7). Nowadays our magnetic sensitivities may have been dulled because of the maelstrom of electromagnetic fields that surround us, but our ancestors may have been sharply attuned to these fields.

In the first edition of *Places of Power* it remained unresolved as to whether or not magnetic effects at the megaliths could in practice really affect the brain, and therefore cause altered or visionary states of consciousness. This was one of the questions on the present writer's mind when he visited Professor Michael Persinger at Laurentian University, Sudbury, Ontario, in April 1998. Persinger has become famous for,

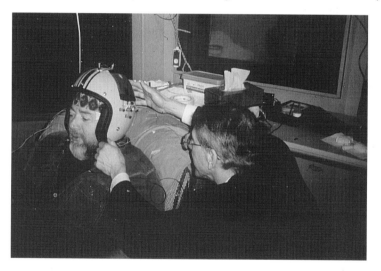

Michael Persinger (left) and assistant wire up the author for a session with the brain/mind-affecting 'magnetic helmet' at Laurentian University. [*Charla Devereux*]

among other things, his 'magnetic helmet' in which a subject has computer-controlled patterns of magnetic waves directed to magnetically-sensitive areas of the brain. Some subjects have reported the sense of 'presences', vivid imagery from childhood, hallucinatory or visionary states, and the appearance of otherworldly beings. Euphoric states can also be generated. However, this all requires modern technology. Could magnetism in megaliths create similar mental effects? Persinger felt that it could. He explained that the technology in his laboratory was needed in order to develop a sufficient effect from a small stimulus in a suitably controlled context. In the case of a 'magnetic megalith', a person could effectively 'bathe' in the different magnetic field provided by the anomaly in the rock. This could affect brain function in some people, causing altered states of consciousness. Persinger also noted that there were factors such as diet that may have made the prehistoric users of the sites particularly sensitive to ambient magnetic fields. In particular, lack of certain nutrients could affect foetal development, resulting in people who had slight changes in their brain structure, rendering them more liable to visionary and mediumistic experiences.

We should at least be open to the possibility that stones containing magnetic anomalies were deliberately employed by the megalith builders to assist in the production of magical, visionary effects at ritual sites. To dismiss it out of hand potentially risks overlooking important information.

THE POWER OF PLACE

The Dragon Project is not, at the time of writing, undertaking physical energy monitoring at sites. Its current concern is to study the effects of selected sites possessing geophysical anomalies on the dreaming mind. Consciousness study is its main concern, for if physical energy effects were deliberately and opportunistically employed at ritual sites, then they were simply one part of an ancient technology of consciousness manipulation that included initiatory ordeals, ritual activity, dancing, drumming, sensory deprivation, the use of drugs—and even the nature of sites themselves. Indeed, much of the otherworldly sensation people experience at ancient sacred places is due to the profound psychological states they can provoke. The aesthetics of a holy place, the play of light and dark, its placing in the topography, even ambient sounds like rushing water or wind in the foliage can all have an effect on the mind of a visitor, especially if already primed to have a spiritual experience.

The opening pages of *Places of Power* emphasize this holistic, traditional sense of 'power', which was usually perceived as being supernatural. The physical anomalies the book goes on to consider comprise only one component of the overall effect an ancient sacred place can provide, and should not be taken out of that context. Nor are such anomalies always present at monumental sites. Nevertheless, with these qualifications, they are factors we should be aware of, and for that reason this new edition of *Places of Power* is timely, allowing the rare collation of information the book contains to be put into circulation once more.

PART ONE

BACKGROUND:
RUMOURS OF POWER

1   TRADITIONS OF POWER

There was a general understanding, prior to the brief centuries of our present culture, that the earth was alive, with subtle but powerful forces flowing through its body, the land. These concentrated at various points that came to be regarded as totemic spots, sacred areas, power places, or temples, depending on the local culture. Each of these locations had its own quality, tutelary deity or 'spirit of place'—*genius loci*. They were points of *geographical sanctity*.

The former inhabitants of our planet roamed their landscapes in cyclic, nomadic patterns. They knew where, when, and how to hunt; where to camp; where best to be at any given season; how to handle and work the natural materials in their environment and what properties they possessed; where to worship the spirits and how to produce mental states that would allow them to enter the magical Otherworld. If illness struck, they knew the procedures and plants that could help (even now pharmacologists have to go to the remaining Indians inhabiting the dwindling rain forests of the world to be educated about the plants in those parts), and by the same token they knew what to ingest to aid in the seeing of visions. They knew what sounds to chant, what images to create, what movements to make, and what postures or exercises to adopt to augment their religious experiences. The shaman or Elders of every tribe knew where to go to have those experiences—which holy ground, cave, spring, peak, or outcrop of rock.

From astronomy to healing and the observation of the spirit world, the knowledge and wisdom of untold generations, obtained from both detailed empirical experience and the deepest recesses of the human psyche, was passed on through a variety of oral and ritual mnemonics. For reasons that are not at all clear, the nomadic, flowing relationship with the land came to an end in Eurasia between about 8,000 and 5,000 years ago. Settlements developed; hunting and gathering gave way over a period of time to agriculture and farming. As if not to forget them, holy places were marked or augmented with earth or stone. New sacred technologies arose. In some cases, the quality of earlier magical caves was reproduced in artificial structures made of large stones ('megalithic') as we shall see in Part Two of this book. The intimate knowledge these ancient people had of the nature and usage of their materials still conjures awe in the modern visitor to the ruins of England's Stonehenge, Ireland's Newgrange, America's Serpent Mound, Peru's Machu Picchu, Egypt's Great Pyramid, or the countless other remarkable works of sacred engineering, large and small, of antiquity.

Sufficient traditional vestiges remain today to illustrate this movement from natural simplicity to sophisticated manipulation.

SITES OF THE DREAMTIME

We can take as an example of the early, natural relationship with the land the various tribes of Australian aborigines who, until recent times, led cyclic nomadic existences in their own lands, moving in annual patterns from one feature to another, tracing a seasonal, geographical course that recreated mythic realities within the spiritual life of the tribe—both an inner and an outer journey.

At points along this journey there were totemic sites. These holy places could be a hill, a waterhole, a large rock, a pavement of quartz, a cave or rocky recess, or a special tree or bush. They were the places where the magical beings of the Dreamtime emerged from the ground, camped, performed a task, or where their forms are preserved in the shape of boulders. Each totemic place had its own song, ceremony and set of sacred objects (called *tapundas*, if wooden, and *tjinas* if made of stone). To the aborigine, these sites were *increase centres*, from which the appropriate ritual could elicit the life essence or *kurunba* of living things, so ensuring the fecundity, the increase, of the particular plant or animal associated with the site. A.P. Elkin (cited in Lévy-Bruhl, 1935), noted that 'Unless the myths...are preserved, the rites performed and the sites maintained as spirit sanctuaries, the living bond is broken, man and nature are separated, and neither man nor nature has any assurance of life in the future'. The anthropologist and explorer, Charles P. Mountford, noted (1968) that the belief in a universal life essence was held by the Walbiri, Ngalia, Aranda, and Pitjandjara aboriginal tribes, and that 'the belief is probably far more widespread than existing literature indicates'. An important site on a totemic route of the Walbiri and Ngalia people is Ngama, a rock outcrop 360 m (400 yd) long by 15 m (60 ft) high near Mount Eclipse in central Australia. Various points and projections on this outcrop, and recesses and caves in it, have mythic significance to the aborigines. A low, isolated rocky hill a few hundred metres west of this outcrop at Ngama was once the camp of Malatji, leader of the mythical dog-people. Every midwinter, tribesmen carry out an increase ritual at a boulder on the west side of this hill, in which an Elder breaks off fragments of its flaking surface. 'This action releases some of the *kurunba* contained in the rock,' Mountford comments, 'which, flying in the air "like a mist" (as the aborigines describe it), fertilizes the female dogs' (*ibid.*). In some ceremonies, dust or stones from a totemic site were thrown into the surrounding area to project ritually the spirit of the place into the landscape.

Of course, the sacred life of the Australian aboriginal has been disrupted, and observances at the sacred places are now only kept up in a relatively fragmentary fashion.

AMERINDIAN SACRED POWER

The Pueblo Indians of south-western USA have very similar understandings to the aborigines, though their social structure took on a more developed nature. Like the Dreamtime entities, the Pueblo people emerged from within the earth, and they feel themselves to be a part of nature; the goal of human existence is to maintain that wholeness. Everything is sacred, so Pueblo shrines tend to blend with the landscape rather than being a place apart, in much the same manner as the aboriginal totemic locations. Rina Swentzell, herself Pueblo Indian, described one such shrine:

Last summer as I stood on Tsikumu, one of Santa Clara Pueblo's sacred mountains, I was most impressed by the wind, the beauty of the clouds and the flow of the hills below. There is a shrine on Tsikumu with a few well-placed stones which define an area scattered with cornmeal and a deeply-worn path in the bedrock. No special structure celebrates the sacredness of this place. Architecturally, it is understated, almost inconspicuous.

Tsikumu is typical of Pueblo shrines in that it is visually disappointing. It is, nevertheless, a special place because it is a place of access to the underworld from which the Pueblo People emerged. It is the doorway of communication between the many simultaneous levels of Pueblo existence. Tsikumu allows for a flow of energy between this plane of reality and other concurrent realities...

The shrines, boundary markers and centers, then, serve as constant reminders of the religious, symbolic nature of life. Because this realm of existence and other realms exist simultaneously, there is a constant flow between levels of existence. Because the *nan-sipu* (center) is the symbolic point from which the people emerged, the shrines (as at Tsikumu) are points where the possibility for contact with different levels of existence happen.

Like the Australian aborigines, the Pueblo Indians also recognize a life essence. They call it *Po-wa-ha*, which translates as 'water-wind-breath'. Swentzell states: 'It is the breath which flows without distinction through the entirety of animate and inanimate existences' (*ibid.*). *Po-wa-ha* thus flows through places as well as people, animals, and plants.

Other Indian tribes had similar ideas. The universal life essence to the Iroquois was *orenda*; to the Sioux it was *waken* or *wakonda*; and to the Crows it was *maxpe*.

THE POWER SYSTEMS OF OLD CHINA

The meaning of *Po-wa-ha* is strikingly similar to that for the ancient Chinese system of geomancy or sacred geography—Feng shui, which means 'wind and water'. Though the Chinese concept of natural forces or energies was sophisticated and complex, the basic similarity of the ideas is recognizable in the comments of a Victorian missionary to China, Ernest J. Eitel (1973):

> They [Feng shui geomants] see a golden chain of spiritual life running through every form of existence and binding together, as one living body, everything that subsists in heaven above or on earth below. What has so often been admired in the natural philosophy of the Greeks—that they made nature live; that they saw in every stone, in every tree, a living spirit; that they peopled the sea with naiads, the forest with satyrs—this poetical, emotional and reverential way of looking at natural objects, is equally so a characteristic of natural science in China.

Feng shui, as it has come down to us, was practised from at least early medieval times, and there is evidence indeed that its principles were being used up to 3,000 years ago in China. No dwelling or tomb would be built without a Feng shui geomant or *hsien-sheng* studying the site and making necessary adjustment to the flow of energies there. As Eitel explained (*ibid.*):

> there are in the earth's crust two different, shall I say magnetic, currents, the one male, the other female; the one positive, the other negative... The one is allegorically called the azure dragon, the other the white tiger...This therefore is the first business of the geomancer on looking out for a propitious site, to find a true dragon, and its complement the white tiger, both being discernible by certain elevations of the ground...in the angle formed by dragon and tiger, in the very point where the two (magnetic) currents which they individually represent cross each other, there may the luck-bringing site, the place for a tomb or dwelling, be found...there must be there also a tranquil harmony of all

the heavenly and terrestrial elements which influence that particular spot, and which is to be determined by observing the compass and its indication of the numerical proportions, and by examining the direction of the water courses.

The Feng shui compass, or *luopan*, is a complex affair, consisting of a central, magnetic compass needle surrounded by numerous circuits of symbols representing a range of conditions and aspects that had to be balanced together in the optimum case of site divination. The dragon and tiger symbols represented, respectively, the *yang* and *yin* forces within the earth, discernible by topography. These masculine and feminine principles occur throughout all creation in ancient Chinese cosmology, as in many others—the first principles emerging from the godhead, Tao, or whatever else one chooses to call the undifferentiated Divine Ground of existence.

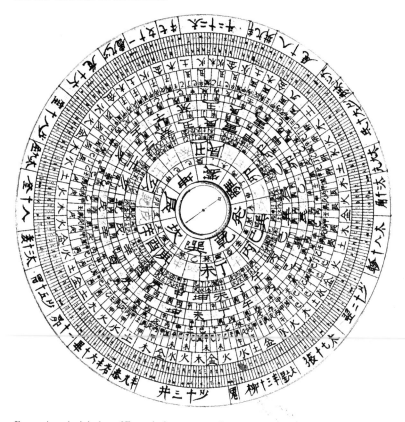

FIG. 1 A typical design of Feng shui compass or *luopan*.

Two basic schools of Feng shui developed over the centuries: one concerned itself primarily with the actual lie of the land, while the other dealt with more abstract correspondences between philosophical and astrological principles. But in all cases, the key matter was the state of *ch'i* at a site. *Ch'i*, like *po-wa-ha* and *kurunba*, was considered to be a kind of universal essence or force, a 'cosmic breath' or 'life breath' that sustains all things. It operates at different scales. Acupuncture was the system developed to study and influence *ch'i* for human health; at the landscape level the system was Feng shui. There are various *ch'i* in the heavens and earth, and an optimum balance of these was attempted at a site. In mountainous terrain, *ch'i* would rush vigorously; in flat, monotonous country it would become sluggish, stagnant. Feng shui not only catalogued these characteristics, it also attempted to influence or control *ch'i*. So actual topographical modifications might be made at a location, with landscape engineering altering the slope of a hillside, for example. Similarly, water courses might be modified, trees planted, hollows scooped out of the ground, fountains or ponds installed. (Water carried *ch'i* and could be used to attract or contain it in an area—rushing, radiating, straight streams at a location, by the same token, would tend to disperse any *ch'i*.) Straight features—roads, water courses, ridges, rows and avenues of trees, railway lines, embankments, lines of posts, and so on—were 'secret arrows', causing *ch'i* to rush along them. A straight line pointing at a dwelling, for example, would bring harmful influences into the home and had to be deflected, screened against or else mitigated by the judicious placing of a water feature. A straight line running at right angles across the frontage of a house was also bad, because it would drain away the site's *ch'i* along its course. The obtaining of the right amount of *ch'i* at a site, in a balanced, harmonious condition, was the aim of the exercise. Too much, too little, too vigorous, too sluggish—all these *ch'i* states had to be avoided. As Stephen Skinner has pointed out (1982): 'The essence of good feng-shui is to trap the ch'i energy flowing through the site and accumulate it without allowing it to go stagnant'.

(Interestingly, while the populace avoided straight-line features under guidance of Feng shui principles, the emperor in the Forbidden City at Beijing conducted his formal business on a throne situated at the focus of linear features, the most notable being the marbled meridian, the cosmic axis of the city. This apparent paradox actually yields some important clues regarding the mystery of straight-line geomancy, of which the ley enigma is a part, and is discussed at length elsewhere—see Pennick and Devereux, 1989.) Straight lines and other inauspicious aspects of a site, such as corridors of cold, blustery winds or poor soil, for example, create conditions producing a negative form of *ch'i*, called *sha*, as Skinner (1982) further explains:

FIG. 2 A Feng shui geomancer at work studying a site for a city.

Sha is the antithesis of ch'i and can be translated as 'noxious vapour'. It is a form of evil ch'i and is often called sha ch'i or feng sha (noxious wind).

Sha can be produced by a configuration of the landform which leads to the loss of good ch'i or actively promotes evil ch'i, or it can be generated by conflicting influences and conjunctions as determined by the compass. It can literally refer to a cold wind issuing from the earth.

Feng shui has officially been discontinued in mainland China, but it blossoms still in such places as Hong Kong, Singapore, and Taiwan. The Feng shui we now see is a hotch-potch of authentic esoteric matter, common sense based on a close observation of the natural world, and rules and superstitions that have arisen for various reasons that have nothing to do with genuine principles of geomancy. An example of the latter is the Feng shui dictum that states that a narrow frontage on a house brings good luck: Evelyn Lip shows (1979) that this notion is a survival of a time when taxes on houses were assessed on their width!

A large part of Feng shui terminology actually defines effects rather than causes, so *sha*, for example, is perceived less as a specific kind of force than as an inauspicious aspect of a site arising from a range of different conditions, as noted above. We shall encounter a modern term for *sha* later in this book.

The world is subject to quite different conditions and problems today, compared with those in old China (the electromagnetic environment, modern building materials, large-scale ecological effects of human activity, and so on), and it is wholly inappropriate for classical ideas of Feng shui, complete with its now outmoded superstitions and local Chinese nuances and obsessions, to be simply plastered onto late twentieth-century circumstances elsewhere in the world, as seems to be the vogue in certain Western 'New Age' circles today. Nevertheless, if we cut through the superstitious or now irrelevant parts of Feng shui, and attempt to see beyond what is to us rather colourful allegorical imagery and terminology, we can see that the core of the system is based on an intimate understanding of nature. And behind what are undoubtedly sophisticated insights into geological, meteorological, medical, and architectural matters, Feng shui identifies precisely the same kind of forces or energies as we find referred to by the Indians of the American south-west or the aborigines of the Australian Outback.

OTHER NAMES OF POWER

People outside of those continents also recognized an essential force or life essence. To the Pacific Islanders it was *mana*, a force that occupied living and inanimate things. Its similarity to concepts of *kurunba*, *ch'i*, or *po-wa-ha* is evident in this description of *mana* by William Howells (1948):

> It was the basic force of nature through which everything was done...The comparison of mana with electricity, or physical energy, is here inescapable. The Polynesian conception of it was not scientific, of course, but it was otherwise completely logical. Mana was believed to be indestructible, although it might be dissipated by improper practices...It flowed continuously from one thing to another and, since the cosmos was built on a dualistic idea, it flowed from heavenly things to earthbound things, just as though from a positive to a negative pole...
>
> Mana could be contained in any person or thing...Chiefs were the main vessels, acting as contacts between god and man...And, since mana flowed from high to low, an unguarded contact between a chief and a commoner was therefore an evil thing; the chief suffered a loss of mana...and the commoner, with his limited capacity for mana, might be blown out like a fuse...
>
> Tabu is another idea which, like mana, the Polynesians thought out carefully, and from which they have given us the word (properly tapu) for our own use...
>
> Tabu was, in Polynesian philosophy, an upset, or anything that caused an upset, in the proper balance of mana.

In North Africa, the force is known as *baraka*; to the ancient Greeks it was *pneuma*; to the Hindus, *prana*. Everywhere we look, earlier peoples had the concept of a force, or certain classes of energies, that moved through all things, and informed the living with vitality, with life. It could be accumulated and controlled to some extent, and esoteric technologies were developed to this end. To modern Western culture, such ideas are simply old superstitions, of no value outside that of religious history, folklore, and, possibly, anthropology. In no area of our intellectual establishment would we find any acceptance that something *actual* might be involved in these primary concepts. But a cynic of such cultural arrogance might point out that never before has the human race come so close to destroying its planetary habitat...

There is no doubt that many of these ideas are suffused with superstitions and, where still extant, have become somewhat degenerate, similar to the relationship of today's popular newspaper horoscope with serious astrology.

2 THE MODERN QUEST

Today, when we walk in the landscape, our science tells us that we move through invisible seas of geomagnetism, natural radiation, and gravity variations. We have a good general understanding of the way these things behave on earth, though there are crucial gaps in our knowledge and, as I shall argue later, we do not have a clear picture of how they act on a small scale at specific points in the landscape. There can be little doubt that some of the attributes accorded to the 'life essence' by former cultures related to the little-known behaviour of some of these now instrumentally measurable natural forces.

In Part Two we see that materials causing the presence of radio-activity, magnetism, and other forces now known to our science were certainly incorporated into the structures of some prehistoric sacred places. But what of those aspects of *ch'i* (or whichever of the other terms one chooses) that seem to relate to some subtler force-field encompassing the electromagnetic spectrum? Can there be a universal force of some kind quietly pulsing beyond the ken of current physical science, yet sensed by early peoples, living closer to nature than we do today? An interpenetrating force that sometimes as a side-effect discloses its presence by causing disturbance in parts of the electromagnetic spectrum?

In relatively recent times various individual researchers have claimed to have discovered such an elusive force. In the first half of the nineteenth century, for instance, Karl von Reichenbach, a German scientist who discovered creosote amongst other things, felt he had identified the universal force: he called it 'Odyle' or 'OD'. He took the name from Wodan, which signified 'the all-penetrating' in Old German—its various idioms as Wuoden, Odan, and Odin were in effect the personification of the all-pervading power of the godhead. By using sensitives or psychics who could see auras or fields round objects in controlled tests, he eventually felt able to claim the force existed, that it had polarity, and that it travelled or flowed through metal conductors at about 90 cm (40 in) per second, which is too fast for conducting heat and too slow for electricity and magnetism. His findings seem to have been confirmed in the early twentieth century by

Dr E. Boirac in France, who managed to use instrumentation to some extent.

Roughly a century after Reichenbach, the Austrian Wilhelm Reich came up with 'orgone energy'. In his early career a distinguished Freudian analyst, Reich committed the sin of searching for physical evidence of the 'life force' (as he called it), trespassing on areas outside his field of psychology. His research led him to announce that he had identified this universal energy, and that it could be accumulated in boxes made of alternating layers of organic and inorganic materials. Peering into the darkness within such boxes, a dull green dance of energy could be seen, moving in characteristic spiral formations. When Reich claimed that this accumulated orgone could be used for weather control and healing, he brought the full wrath of orthodoxy down onto his head, and he died in an American jail in 1957.

It is hard to judge whether such people as these were a little mad or actually onto something worthwhile. Even though 'respectable' science continues to search slyly for its ether, its unified field, its 'Fifth Force' beyond the known ones of gravity, electromagnetism, and the weak and strong nuclear forces, our culture does not readily condone research into such things, and those independent souls who persist in doing so tend to become isolated, ridiculed, resisted, and—perhaps eventually—sent crazy. It is certainly at least a coincidence, however, as John Michell noted years ago, that the structure of certain prehistoric mounds were also constructed from alternating organic and inorganic layers, much like Reich's orgone accumulators:

> it is difficult not to suspect that this form of energy [orgone] was known and controlled in prehistoric times. Many of the greatest works of the megalithic builders involved the construction of a hidden chamber set deep within the earth or at the heart of some great artificial edifice...The chamber itself is lined with stone covered with a layer of turf and with successive layers of clay and sod. These layers are carefully built up, different types and colours of clay being used at each stage. Finally the whole structure is buried under a great mound of earth.
>
> (Michell, 1969)

FIG. 3 Drawing showing the deliberate layering of material revealed when an archaeological trench was cut into the side of the Irish Neolithic mound of Knowth.

21

PLATE 1 Silbury Hill, the largest artificial mound in Europe, built from chalk and earth.

The mound of Knowth, in the Boyne Valley north of Dublin, was certainly stratified, being built from 'alternating layers of stones, boulder clay and shale' on a bed of redeposited sods (Eogan, 1986). The great artificial mound of Silbury in Wiltshire, the largest man-made mound in all prehistoric Europe, was constructed from chalk and soil.

22

ENIGMAS OF STONE AND EARTH

It is the ancient monuments of the British Isles that are primarily the concern of this book, because that is where most of the energy studies of sites have been carried out to date. Also, while the aborigines, Amerindians, and other societies around the world had subtlely marked or even wholly natural sacred sites, the British and Continental European ceremonial places of the Neolithic ('New Stone') and Bronze Ages (fourth to second millennia BC in Britain, and earlier in other parts of Europe) display more engineered ways of marking—and perhaps *creating*—a place of power. At these monuments we are in the presence of *technology*, the impressive remains left by a group of races who were the founders of what has become today's 'Western culture', which has put its stamp, indeed has stamped, over most of the world. At these places we catch that first concerted wave of collective technological effort, an effort that accompanied the first use of farming and the occurrence of settlement. Frozen in structures of earth and stone, we have a record of the curious 'moment' in our history when some profound alteration in consciousness took place, and the dreaming, cyclic journey across the earth was halted and the processes that led directly to our current state of cultural consciousness was commenced. Something changed.

We catch this 'spiritual technology', to use Michell's phrase, when it was still informed by a profound reverence for the earth; when the soil and rock of the land, its flora, fauna, energies, and processes were intimately understood and directly experienced. When the urge to affect the environment in order to control certain conditions or to gain access to particular advantages was poised in a delicate balance between the knowledge and memory of generations and the commencement of that helter-skelter of technological innovation and scientific discovery that has brought us to the global spiritual, social and ecological crises we face at the end of the second millennium AD.

By studying these places, and by considering them in a frame a little wider than that used solely by archaeology, can we return to that moment, can we regain certain understandings that have been lost, or perhaps only forgotten? Understandings that might help us regain our balance inwardly, spiritually, and psychologically, and outwardly in terms of ecology? How to give our spirituality a place in the landscape is also a problem as yet barely addressed by today's ecological activists.

It is a daunting task. While active, living vestiges of traditions and geomantic systems still linger in other parts of the world, we have no direct links with the builders of the stone and earth monuments that are left to us from the prehistory of Europe. Only the awesome, gaunt, silent structures themselves—some of them old before the Egyptian pyramids were built—offer us a possible bridge back across the millennia to the minds of their builders.

FOLK MEMORY

We first have to look at what exists of oral, and subsequently written, lore in the hope that actual recall of the megalithic technology may be partially contained within it, however fragmented and distorted.

Such writers as the Frenchman, Louis Charpentier (1966), and the Belgian, Pierre Méreaux (1981), remind us of the *Wouivre* or *Nwyvre*, the 'fifth element' of the Iron Age Druids, who saw the closing chapters of prehistory in Europe, and were ultimately driven into extinction. Méreaux explains (*ibid.*).

> For the Ancients, the world was composed of four elements: water, earth, air and fire, which are none other than the three states of matter (liquid, solid, and gaseous), fire or heat being what was 'added' to pass from one state to another. The Druids added a fifth element, *Nwyvre*, contained in all the others and in which they saw an image of the universal structure of matter and a symbol of God. The exact physical nature of the *Nwyvre* is not very clear, and neither the ancient Gaulish texts, nor Druidic tradition shed any light on this...
>
> *Nwyvre* is translated as 'ether, celestial matter, penetrating element'...the name itself, which is very curious...comes from the Indo-European root *wed*, meaning water, and which is also the origin of the Greek word *hudros* (water serpent), which became 'hydre' in French and is the mother of all our words composed with hydr or hydro. In Old French, *guivre* or *vivre* meant 'serpent' until the fifteenth century and it is still used with this same meaning in heraldry. And, under Germanic influence, this root *wed* became 'vobero' or 'vabero' in Gaulish— underground water. As we can see, everything turns round the image of the serpent, a most wave-like animal, and underground water...it is...undeniable that this *Nwyvre* has left deeply rooted traces in our place names...And, in Old German and in English, 'wabern' and 'waver' are translated as oscillating...
>
> And it may also be related to all our popular legends that are crawling with dragons and underground serpents, symbols of unknown forces, spitting fire and lightning, and which are undoubtedly memories of a residual symbolic survival of *Nwyvre*.

It seems as if we have encountered yet again our old friends, *ch'i*, *kurunba*, *po-wa-ha*, and the rest, in another guise. We do not know if the notion of *Nwyvre* originated in the Iron Age, or whether the Druids were guardians of much older traditions, but it may be of significance to note an interesting image carved on a stone in the remarkable Neolithic chambered mound on the island of Gavrinis, off the coast of Brittany near Larmor Baden. Here all the stones, except one quartz block, shimmer with the most fantastic linear designs, said by archaeologists to represent features such as goddess images in highly abstracted style.

One of the stones lining the north-east side of the entrance passage has three very distinct, serpent-like oscillating lines, rising, it seems, out of the ground at the base of the stone. It is difficult not to think of this as a most graphic depiction of the *Nwyvre* or earth power.

The *Nwyvre* is as close as we can get to explicit information about north-west European traditions of power in prehistory. For any other hints we have to resort to legends that were committed to writing

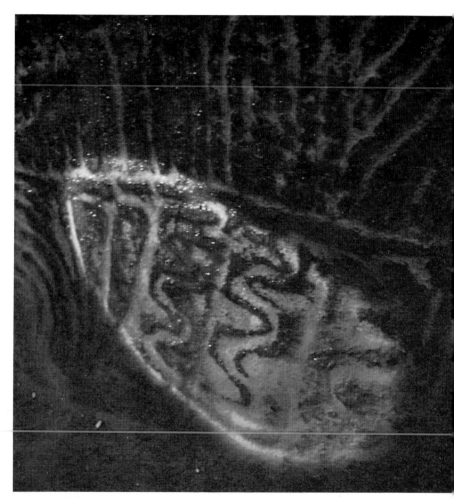

PLATE 2 A flashlight reveals *Nwyvre* markings snaking up out of the ground on the base of a stone in the Neolithic chambered mound of Gavrinis, Brittany.

25

mainly in recent centuries, and we can only hazard a guess as to how long they existed in oral form prior to that. If we look at British folklore specifically related to prehistoric sites, we can discern perhaps thirteen basic legendary motifs that could possibly be of considerable antiquity, relating to a folk recognition of there being certain sites with curious properties.

HEALING

Healing is mainly associated with stones and water. The classic megalithic example is Men-an-Tol in Cornwall. Children suffering from rickets (a disorder causing fragile or soft bones) or 'crick in the neck' would be passed three or nine times through the stone's hole. In some versions, the patient was drawn three times along the grass around the stone against the sun (widdershins). Adults with rheumatic conditions would also seek healing at the stone by climbing through the hole. Several other holed stones around the country had similar traditions. The stones of Stonehenge also supposedly had healing properties, obtained by splashing water on them and making a bath or infusion from the liquid. Many standing stones were considered effective in healing.

Certain holy wells were also thought to have healing properties—the taking of the waters could be good for a wide range of ailments, though 'sore eyes' seems to have been the major condition treated! While these may not be thought to be prehistoric sites, most authorities agree that many of these wells and springs were venerated in at least late prehistoric times, the process simply becoming Christianized later. Indeed, the veneration of water is likely to have come down from remotest antiquity.

MOVEMENT

Movement is specifically associated with stones. Variations on the theme are that a particular standing stone or set of stones would go down to a nearby stream to drink, or run around the field, or rise up out of the ground and rotate 'when they hear a clock strike midnight', 'when the cock crows', 'at noon', or at particular times of the year, such as All Hallows. Folklorist Leslie Grinsell (1976) humorously points out that the Hoarstone, near Enstone, Oxfordshire, is supposed to go to drink when it hears the church clock at Lidstone strike midnight, yet Lidstone church does not have a striking clock!

A counter-theme of this motif is that certain stones cannot be moved by human agency or, if they are so displaced, will either return automatically or else cause such problems that the person involved will

PLATE 3 Men-an-Tol, the holed stone, Cornwall. Formerly used for healing and as an oracle.

PLATE 4 The Enstone Hoarstone lurks within its grove, secure in the knowledge that if it is removed, it will return by itself. It goes for a drink when the Lidstone church clock strikes midnight on Midsummer Eve.

feel obliged to return the stone, and will find it supernaturally easy to do so. An interesting aspect of these legends is that some stones that move magically by themselves at appointed times, are also ones that resist displacement by humans. A case in point is the Enstone Hoarstone that, it is said, will return of its own accord if moved.

PETRIFACTION

Stones at numerous sites, according to this theme, are people who have been turned to stone, usually for working, playing, or otherwise transgressing the Sabbath. An example is the stone circle complex at Stanton Drew, Avon. The stones here were members of a wedding party whose dancing and partying went on through the night and into Sunday. The hired fiddler declined to continue after midnight, but a stranger appeared who offered to play on until dawn. This was, naturally, the Devil. The people were duly turned to stone, and will only be released from their petrological bondage when the Devil comes to play for them again. Janet and Colin Bord, making a general point about the folklore of ancient sites, rightly observed (1976) that this theme 'is by no means peculiar to the British Isles, but is repeated in many parts of the world, even the remotest areas'. We can see this to be true in this instance, because a stone circle near Kaur, in the Senegambian area of western Africa, is similarly supposed to be a bridal party turned to stone (Castle, 1979).

COUNTLESS STONES

Grinsell (1976) notes that this theme was attached to at least eleven stone circles or other megalithic structures in Britain. The legends state that the stones at these places cannot be properly counted. Each time one tries, a different number will be arrived at. Folklore records that certain individuals, in an attempt to circumvent this frustrating situation, would take a given number of loaves to a site, and place one on each stone, with the aim of counting the loaves left. However, the Devil always spoiled such attempts by surreptitiously knocking the placed loaves to the ground.

GIANT ASSOCIATIONS

Many megaliths or large natural boulders are said, in folklore, to have been placed in their positions by giants of old. Prehistoric earthen or stone mounds have also attracted similar legends. A Neolithic chambered mound on Anglesey has the name Barclodiad-y-Gawres, which means 'the apronful of the giantess'. Identical legends also involve the

PLATE 5 The southernmost stone of the Devil's Arrows. At 6.4 m (21 ft) it is the tallest of the three surviving megaliths. Legend says the stones were arrows shot by the Devil, which fell short of their target. This 'bow-shot' image could be a folk memory of a geomantic aspect to the site: the stones lie on at least two alignments (leys), which are very well attested to cartographically, archaeologically, and statistically.

PLATE 6   Stonehenge, Wiltshire, viewed from Station Stone 91, to the south-east.

Devil, presumably a Christianized version of the pre-existing giant theme. The three surviving megaliths called the Devil's Arrows near Boroughbridge in North Yorkshire speak for themselves.

Two giant themes are associated with Stonehenge: it was once known as the 'Giants Dance', and the bluestones came originally from Africa via Ireland. A deep memory may be contained in that legend. Giant associations with sites is another motif echoed thousands of miles away in Africa, for in The Gambia, tradition states that the stone circles at Sanguli were 'built by ancient people who were eight metres tall'.

DESECRATION

As if a curse has been left guarding them, it is said of many prehistoric sites that bad luck or death will befall anyone disturbing them. There are many traditions to this effect, and numerous anecdotal accounts that claim people actually have experienced misfortune after destroying a site.

PLATE 7 Carreg-y-Bucci, or Hobgoblin Stone, near Lampeter, Wales.

A fascinating sub-theme of this motif makes an enigmatic link between some monuments and meteorology: people disturbing these sites can expect to be subjected to severe weather conditions such as freak winds or fierce electrical storms. Again, there are a considerable number of accounts of this actually happening. In 1849, for instance, when Dean Merewether of Hereford and his team were digging at Silbury Hill near Avebury in Wiltshire, a 'dramatic high Gothick thunderstorm' broke out, and men working deep within the great mound felt it shudder to its base. The Dean wryly observed that the significantly timed storm was 'much to the satisfaction...of the rustics'. A farmer told Lewis Edwards in the 1940s that when he approached Carreg-y-Bucci (the Hobgoblin Stone)—on top of a prehistoric mound near Lampeter, Wales—with the intention of breaking it up for gateposts, 'there was a violent thunderstorm, the worst I have ever known. I ran for my life, but it followed me all the way home'. Three men had been killed by lightning alongside the stone (Edwards, 1949).

31

FAIRIES

Fairies and other elemental entities were traditionally thought to inhabit particular prehistoric sites. These places were usually mounds, but megaliths were sometimes involved (the Humber Stone, Leicestershire, for example). A classic fairy site is Willy Howe, Humberside—a large Neolithic mound that from at least medieval times was considered a fairy mound. Travellers passing that way at night would be on their guard if they heard the sounds of revelry coming from the barrow. In the twelfth century, William of Newburgh recorded that a local countryman saw an opening in the mound one night and on peering in saw a fairy banquet in progress. He was offered a cup of wine, but the man knew better than to drink or eat fairy food or enter the magically illuminated fairy domain, lest he become enchanted. We might say in today's terminology that that would mean he would experience a time warp, the 'Rip Van Winkle effect', often reported by UFO abductees (modern fairylore). He threw away the drink but ran off with the cup, much to the outrage of the fairies. The cup was said to be of unknown material, of an unusual colour and shape, and to have passed into the possession of Henry the Elder.

As will become clear by the end of the present book, *lights* were also seen at some ancient sites, and these undoubtedly were referred to as fairies by countryfolk. Nowhere was this habit stronger than in Ireland. The Irish writer, Dermot Mac Manus, gives as one example the prehistoric earthworks or 'fairy forts' near Castlebar, County Mayo. 'The first fort is called Crillaun,' Mac Manus writes (1973),

> and in the neighbourhood it has always been known to be a busy centre of fairy activity. From time to time the fort has been seen ablaze with little winking lights. They are said to move from one fort to another sometimes, though this is rare.

Mac Manus goes on to interview local people who claim to have actually witnessed the lights on one or two occasions. Lights only are seen—the fairy designation is purely a cultural reflex. Similarly, in Cornwall in the nineteenth century, tin miners returning from work claimed to have seen 'lights burning and fairies dancing on and around' the Carn Gluze round barrow on the coast at St Just.

TREASURE

Mounds and stone circles were frequently reported to contain treasure. Willy Howe also had this legend attached to it. The story goes that people dug into the mound to reach a chest of gold. They attached a chain and horses to it, but the harder the animals pulled, the deeper the chest sank into the barrow. An almost identical tale is attached to

PLATE 8 The wooded fairy mound of Neolithic Willy Howe was also said to contain treasure.

another prehistoric barrow, Mutlow Hill in Essex, the treasure there being a golden coach. A great many other sites around the country are said to conceal treasure. In some cases, dragons guarded hoards of riches.

Lights figure again in treasure lore. In many countries, in Europe and South America particularly, curious lights that appear repeatedly at intervals in the same area, are said to mark the position of buried treasure. Denmark had a strong tradition of these treasure lights, at least until the turn of the century, and in Germany if treasure is buried at a ruined site, blue flames or globes of light mark the location. These lights can turn into animal spirits, which can mutilate any human unwise enough to start digging for the treasure. 'Very often,' writes Ulrich Magin in *The Ley Hunter* (1988),

> the gold is disguised as something ordinary; grains of wheat, leaves, bones or even excrement. The finder throws this away, only to find, the very next day, that the few remains left have turned into gold. This could be a hint that some kind of different wealth is involved here.

In Peru, treasure lights are called *la loz del dinero* ('the money lights') and in Brazil *Mae de Ouro* (Mother of Gold). In Cornwall, the Iron Age earthworks on Trencrom Hill are supposed to harbour giants' treasure. It is said that a tin miner two hundred or so years ago saw lights on the hill and climbed up to find a long passage, along which was unguarded gold. Interestingly, it was traditional amongst medieval miners of copper, tin, and other metals to look for light phenomena emerging from the ground, as that was said to indicate the presence of good veins of ore (Devereux, 1989).

In keeping an eye on comparable themes elsewhere, it is to be noted that in Senegambia once more—where there are over 800 stone circles, nearly as many as in the British Isles—a bag of gold was held by a genie that manifested out of a stone at one of the Sanguli circles. If anyone went to take the bag, it and the genie would simply melt back into one of the stones.

GHOSTS

It is almost to be expected that some folklore would claim that there were spectres at ancient places. These are usually castles and old houses, but some have been associated with prehistoric sites. A particularly interesting legend involves the apparition of a gigantic golden figure seen at the barrow of Bryn-yr-Ellyllon (the Hill of Goblins) near Mold in North Wales. This old story seems to have pre-dated the finding of a gold corselet found when the mound was cleared in 1833. If this is in fact the case, then it would seem that relatively specific memories can be encapsulated in lore down a great many generations.

A phantom horseman was seen near a round barrow on Bottlebush Down in Dorset in the winter of 1927–8 by the archaeologist, Dr R.C.C. Clay. A person who rested on a nearby barrow on another occasion suddenly found himself surrounded by 'little people in leather jerkins', and a shepherd also saw a phantom horseman appear from behind a clump of shrubs near a prehistoric earthwork on the down (Harte, 1986; Pennick and Devereux, 1989). (Bottlebush Down is crossed by one of the largest and most enigmatic earthworks of the Neolithic period—a six-mile-long *cursus*, formed by parallel lines of ditches and banks, now almost invisible at ground level.)

Lights have been associated in folk tradition with spirits and ghosts at prehistoric features. Six independent witnesses told antiquarian G. Wilson in the 1880s that they saw, on repeated occasions, a light move from Torhouskie Cairn in Scotland to a stone on top of a water conduit. The stone supposedly had been taken from the cairn, so the light was 'claiming its own'. The old Scandinavians would not have been surprised: 'lambent flames' issuing from burial cairns were a part of their folklore, and they had a name for them—*haug-eldir*.

PLATE 9 Some of the haunted Bronze Age round barrows on Bottlebush Down, Dorset.

Given one context or another by the rural mentality, by folklore, strange lights and ancient sites clearly seem to have enjoyed some kind of association. We see in Part Two that they still do.

DIVINATION

Holy wells were often used for prophecy (oracular usage), but it seems some megaliths may also have shared this role, if the fragment of tradition still surviving with regard to Men-an-Tol, the Cornish holed stone famed for healing (above), is anything to go by: it was said that brass pins placed across one another on top of the stone would acquire a curious motion and the answer to a question addressed to the stone could be deciphered by the movements of the pins.

NUMBER

Grinsell (1976) has noted that 'Customs still (or recently) practised at most prehistoric sites usually involve the numbers three, seven or nine'.

In addition to such customs, these numbers become attached to sites in other ways: for example, a group of prehistoric mounds being called 'Seven Barrows', when there are, in fact, many more in the cluster.

HIDDEN PASSAGES

Some sites are said to have underground tunnels leading from them, usually going to some other feature. In Leicestershire, the Humber Stone (now just a stump) was said to have a tunnel connecting it with the former St John's Stone in Abbey Fields, Leicester, about 5 km (3 miles) away. There is no physical tunnel, and such motifs in folklore are often taken to imply folk memory of an alignment or other connection between sites. In the case of the supposed Humber Stone tunnel, the local historian, Dryden, suggested as long ago as 1911 that it was the memory of an astronomical line, as she claimed that the midsummer sun would have been visible rising behind the Humber

PLATE 10 The remains of Coldrum Barrow, a Neolithic site on an alignment recalled in legend as a 'tunnel'. Likewise, the still-visible old straight tracks laid down by the lost Anasazi people in the desert around Chaco Canyon, New Mexico, are regarded in Navajo folk stories as tunnels along which the Anasazi could invisibly travel.

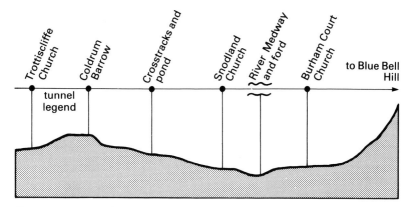

FIG. 4   An alignment is found formed by ancient sites across the Kentish countryside if the line of the 'tunnel' claimed in folklore to link Trottiscliffe church with Coldrum Barrow is extended [*Ian Thomson*].

Stone when viewed from the St John's Stone. And Alfred Watkins, the father of leys (or 'ley lines'), suggested that the motif indicated the existence of an alignment of sites, a 'ley line' as they are often referred to nowadays. This seems to be the case at the Neolithic Coldrum Barrow in Kent, where a tunnel is said to link it with the nearby church of SS Peter and Paul at Trottiscliffe (Trosley). This legend in fact marks an alignment that can be traced for over 6.5 km (4 miles), running: Trosley church–Coldrum Barrow–Snodland church–ancient ford at River Medway–Burham Court church (Devereux and Devereux, 1986). Trosley church has megaliths embedded in its Saxon foundations.

FERTILITY

Fertility is associated with some stones, in terms of the fertility of humans, animals, and crops. At the quartz monolith known as the White Lady of Ballafreer on the Isle of Man, a woman about to be married would hold water from a nearby well in her mouth and walk three times round the stone invoking the Trinity before swallowing the water. This was supposed to promote fertility. Newly-weds would hold hands and circumambulate the Kempock Stane near Gourock in Scotland asking for fruitful union. The Cornish Tolven Stone was said to not only heal sickly infants, but also to ensure fertility in a person if he or she crawled naked through the hole in it. Janet and Colin Bord (1982) note that young couples would exchange betrothal vows at the stones at Callanish on the Isle of Lewis and that, moreover, it was said to be 'an auspicious place to consummate a marriage'. Certain holed

FIG. 5 The Tolven Stone, Cornwall, associated with both healing and fertility traditions.

stones, such as the former Stone of Odin on Orkney or the Stone of Doagh in Northern Ireland, were used by engaged couples to clasp hands through as a sign of contract. A barren sow could be cured if a healer touched it through the hole in a stone at Caherurlagh, County Cork, Ireland (*ibid.*). In Lincolnshire, a stone was beaten to promote good crops, while on the Isle of Skye people would bow to the former Bowing Stone for the same purpose. At the Neolithic effigy stone, known as La Gran'mère du Chimquière on Guernsey, fruits and flowers would be left to ensure good luck and fertility. Some stones were thought to be able to produce rainfall in order to help the growth of crops.

There are, of course, other aspects of folklore attached to prehistoric sites (Grinsell, 1976, identifies almost thirty), but the others have motifs certainly or probably originating in the historic era—associations with King Arthur, etymological explanations for sites, Christianization, assemblies, and such like.

Folklore was the mnemonic of simple countryfolk; it was designed to be used at the rural hearth on dark winter evenings, to help explain the mysterious stones and earthworks with which these people shared the landscape. While rulers came and went, the peasant population remained fairly intact, until the great scattering caused by the Industrial Revolution. Even today, folklore is still passed on in areas that have retained some degree of rural integrity. Legends are like time capsules, and germs of truth can be conveyed within elaborate imagery and story-telling. It is just conceivable that the thirteen themes outlined above contain hints of genuine information if they can be deciphered.

The ideas that stones can move in a variety of ways, that they are petrified people, and that they can evade being counted, suggest an underlying sense that the stones have something *animate* about them. This is endorsed by other lore claiming stones can grow. The stones are alive in some way, even if not in the literal sense.

The various themes dealing with fairies, ghosts, lights, and enchantment suggest the underlying observations of generations of local people that unusual phenomena have been seen or associated with stone circles and similar places. We will shortly see that this is still the case.

Healing traditions also attest to the belief in certain stones having qualities about them that can beneficially affect the human organism. Modern medicine now accepts that low-level electromagnetic therapy can help healing in certain medical conditions—especially bone disorders. In Part Two we see that at least some of the megaliths studied do possess quite definite magnetic and other energetic properties. The fertilizing capacity of some stones was probably closely linked to the healing theme (the Tolven Stone has both traditions associated with it, for example), and bears close similarity with the Australian aborigine concept of 'increase centres'. This association with standing stones was graphically announced in some cases, where the phallic-like nature of monoliths was explicitly depicted. In the graveyard of Aghowle church in County Wicklow, Ireland, for instance, is a 1.5-m (5-ft) stone in the form of a phallus (though its glans has now been destroyed). A similar stone exists at Tømmerby in Denmark, and stone phalli rising to 3m (10 ft) occur near Soddu in southern Ethiopia. Indeed, prehistoric phallic stones occur in several countries.

The weather-affecting aspects of some stones in both fertility and desecration legends are interesting, and may refer to further affects associated with prehistoric features *or their locations*. In general, though, desecration traditions clearly record a sense of site preservation, with a threat or curse to encourage future generations to leave the places intact.

The use of sites as resorts of divination, as oracles, hints at a possible memory relic relating to the production of altered states of consciousness at these places: it is an aspect that will be explored at points in the following pages. The secret-tunnel motif is almost certainly a folk recognition of the relationships of sites one to another in the landscape—their sacred geographic (geomantic) and orientational characteristics. This passageway motif is sometimes linked with the treasure theme, which may in general be a symbol for secret, forgotten aspects of these places that were clearly so important in antiquity—a mnemonic for amnesia, as it were. The numerology that can be linked with sites in various ways may be an authentic memory trace of ritual carried out at the stones and earthworks.

Folklore is highly complex and can rarely be taken at face value: it is eclectic, gathering its images and rationale from many sources. The surface of folklore is regularly repolished and embellished, long after the possible meanings of the fundamental motifs have been forgotten. But it is these legendary cores that are the important components of folklore, and if one sums up those aspects of the themes itemized above, the general sense comes across that the old stones and other places have been regarded as foci of *power*, of unusual—often interpreted as super-natural—phenomena and particular effects. We should not dismiss the folk record too readily.

EARTH MYSTERIES

What has become virtually modern folklore about these sites is that they are 'water marks' located over converging or crossing under-ground streams or springs. This seems to have primarily developed from claims of French dowsers (water diviners or witchers) in the 1930s, and enthusiastically studied in the following two or three decades by such British dowsers as R. Allender Smith and Guy Underwood. These same decades also saw the scientific study of the dowsing faculty, to see if dowsers were responding to ionization, magnetism, or other measurable effects. This work included attempts to photograph 'earth rays'. While some evidence was found to support all of these possibilities, the end results seem to have been inconclusive. The fundamental fact that has emerged, though, is that human beings can be profoundly sensitive to energetic effects in their environment.

Since the 1960s especially, there have been extensions of the dowsing approach to ancient sites, with a plethora of claims that so far unspe-cified 'energies' can also be dowsed at these places. These approaches are outside the scope of this book, but the matter is discussed in a little more detail elsewhere (Pennick and Devereux, 1989).

This dowsing work has, over the last 25 years or so, gone hand in hand with the growth of an extraordinary multi-disciplinary area of enquiry that was given the epithet of 'Earth Mysteries' by an unknown journalist in 1974. Drawing on earlier psychic and physical work at sites, in the 1960s various writers and interested individuals began to develop instinctively a wide-ranging approach to the assessment of megalithic and other prehistoric sites, particularly in Britain. In addition to archaeology itself, the study of folklore, dowsing, astronomical aspects, geomancy, unusual phenomena, and many other strands were brought together in an attempt to obtain as full a picture of these mysterious monuments as possible. This process was founded more on enthusiasm than experience, and considerable naïvety reigned during the 'psychedelic decade'. Negative attitudes towards this fledgling study-area were struck by orthodox disciplines, notably archaeology, partially for understandable reasons, but to some extent also due to arrogance. In subsequent years, the holistic or 'general systems' Earth Mysteries approach to ancient sites and their environments has settled down to more grounded (if still contentious) activity, and various specialist journals and regional groups have become established, if at rather tenuous levels. On the way, much spurious and misinformed material has been disseminated by opportunistic writers and broadcasters, and considerable unfounded opinion and sheer invention has been engendered by 'New Agers' and careless enthusiasts, all of which has confused and clouded the issues and genuine attempts at understanding being addressed by the relatively small number of serious Earth Mysteries researchers.

CRYSTALS

Over the years, certain articles of faith have emerged within Earth Mysteries circles. One of these is the observation that crystals are evident as components of many British megalithic sites, and that this must be significant in some way. The observation is correct to a large degree, though is sometimes exaggerated. Dramatic sites for this aspect are the Callanish group of stone circles on the Isle of Lewis off Scotland's western coast. In the main site of the group, Callanish I, virtually every stone sports a crystal of some sort—white quartz, feldspar, or hornblende. Smaller Callanish sites also have stones shot through with crystalline veins. At the other end of the British Isles, in Cornwall, there is the dramatic Duloe circle, which is comprised of huge megaliths of pure white quartz. Also in Cornwall is the Boscowen-un circle that has one noticeable white quartz block in its circumference. The Harold's Stones in Wales have nuggets of quartz in them, and some stone circles in Wales were originally paved inside with quartz. In Ireland, the mighty Neolithic chambered mound of Newgrange has its eastern walls faced in white quartz, and may once have been entirely covered in the rock. Quartz makes its appearance at many megalithic sites. Even where its presence is not visually apparent,

PLATE 11 The all-quartz stones of the
Duloe circle, Cornwall.

PLATE 12 The single quartz block in
the Boscawen-un circle, Cornwall, can
be seen in this view shining out on the
far side of the ring.

PLATE 13 The three Harold's Stones
near Trellech, Gwent, have white
crystal nuggets peppering their dark
stone.

PLATE 14 A piece of hornblende on a
stone at the main site of the Callanish
group, Callanish I. Most of the stones
at the site sport similar crystals of the
iron silicate.

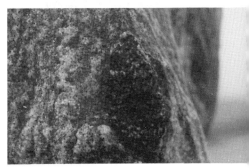

PLATE 15 *Right*: Veins of quartz lace
this stone at Callanish III, Isle of
Lewis.

Earth Mysteries' *aficionados* point out that the stones in many circles are frequently highly crystalline types of rock, such as granite. (I will attempt to demonstrate in later parts of the present book, however, that granite was more likely to have been used by megalith builders for reasons to do with its innate radioactivity.)

If the presence of crystals was deliberate in many cases, what could their function have been? Perhaps just because they look attractive and somehow special? Perhaps because under suitable circumstances quartz can have electrical and vibratory properties? Most likely, the Earth Mysteries researcher would argue, because it had magical or spiritual qualities. There is no doubt at all that many crystals have recorded lore from Roman times at least, and usage from times much earlier. Specific gems were associated with certain properties—healing, promoting sleep, strengthening the heart, offsetting drunkenness, causing invisibility, and many more. Crystals were involved with the esoteric practices of many groups and traditions down the centuries. A property perhaps particularly relevant to ancient sites was that some crystals were said to attract spirits. As W.T. Fernie noted (1907), certain stones 'were supposed to be influenced by the Planets, and to be the abode of spirits'. Various forms of quartz were used for the enhancement of consciousness—rock crystal, for example, was said to be able to induce clairvoyance and was the ideal material for crystal gazing. Quartz was also believed to allow the transduction of spiritual and emotional forces, perhaps an occult corollary of the crystal's ability to transduce physical energies: a voltage passed across a quartz crystal will cause it to vibrate at high frequencies, while a mechanical deformation of a crystal will create electrical charge in it. This capacity to transduce mechanical into electrical energy and vice versa is known as the piezoelectric effect, and has a number of scientific and commercial applications.

This association of crystals, particularly quartz or rock crystal, with spirituality and consciousness seems to have been worldwide, not confined just to Europe and the Middle East. They were a major element in Australian aboriginal initiation practices. In some cases, small pieces of quartz were said to be placed in the initiate's body by supernatural beings; in other instances, Mircea Eliade informs us (1964), the candidate must submit to an operation performed by two elderly medicine men:

> They rub his body with rock crystals to the point of abrading the skin, press rock crystals into his scalp, pierce a hole under a fingernail of his right hand, and make an incision in his tongue...His body is decorated with...lines apparently symbolizing the magical crystals in his body.

To the aborigine, quartz is 'solidified light' that originally came from the sky, and in some initiations the prospective shaman has to drink water that is supposed to be liquified quartz so that he will be filled with light and enabled to 'fly to the sky'. The ability of rock crystal to facilitate shamanistic flight (an image for ecstatic mental states) was also held by some North American Indian tribes. Shamans in Borneo also used 'light stones'—quartz pieces—for clairvoyant purposes.

The ability of crystals to interact with consciousness was thus widely believed in by early peoples, and may be the clue to the repeated occurrence of such material at megalithic sites. I have seen two examples of human–mineral interaction at a prehistoric site, both of them at the Rollright stone circle, Oxfordshire. In one case, during an early morning lull in a 1980 session of the Dragon Project (see below), I handed biologist Harry Oldfield a piece of white quartz I had obtained from Newgrange a short while previously. He attached it to a molecular resonance meter and persuaded Ken Shaw, a psychic we had on site that session, to work with it. Shaw placed his hand a few centimetres from the rock and visualized white light streaming into it. The digital readout on the meter, which was measuring the frequency of the molecular vibration in the crystal sample, began to tumble chaotically. When Shaw stopped visualizing, the readings settled down once more. Shaw was able to repeat this effect every time he tried. A number of other personnel on site at the time literally 'tried their hands' too, many suspecting that it was the proximity of Shaw's hand causing the effect. In fact, no one else could reproduce the effect at all, except one woman who made a slight disturbance in the meter's readout.

Later on that same sunny June day, the Welsh master-dowser, Bill Lewis, joined the Dragon Project team on site. In one of his experiments, he had the tallest stone of the Rollright circle wired to a sensitive voltmeter. The instrument was connected by a cable to the stone, but situated several metres away. It was measuring the millivoltage in the stone and was giving an almost steady reading, with just a right-hand digit lazily changing occasionally. The end of the cable was taped to the stone about four-fifths up its height at a point where Lewis dowsed what he called an 'energy node'. Every time Lewis (who also has a remarkable record as a psychic healer) placed his hands on the node, the readings on the voltmeter scrambled. Time and again, the effect was repeated. Sceptics on site felt that anyone placing their hands there would cause the effect. This was tested, but no one else could affect the instrument's readings. It was then suggested that perhaps coincidental lightning in some distant thunderstorm was inducing an electrical effect in the cable connecting the stone and the voltmeter. We had an electrostatic detector with us, so this suggestion was tested. There was no correlation between bursts of distant static and the dowser's actions.

PLATE 16 Sensitive Ken Shaw psychically affects the molecular vibration in a piece of quartz during a Rollright Dragon Project session, while Harry Oldfield (right) looks on.

PLATE 17 Welsh master-dowser Bill Lewis (centre) affects the voltage in a monitored Rollright stone.

Experiments such as this do not prove anything, but they do provide prima-facie evidence that human beings and minerals can interact in ways that are currently obscure. In his own work, Harry Oldfield has gone on to demonstrate experimentally this potential interaction in greater depth—see Plates 18–20. Though contentious, this type of experimentation may give a hint as to the usage of crystal elements at sacred sites.

The belief in the role of crystals in healing and consciousness work has now become something of a New Age fad, with allusions to the demise of fabled Atlantis being caused by the unwise wielding of 'crystal power'. Much of this current fad is nonsensical, even though it may have some actual basis, distorted by time and modern superficiality. It is sad to learn of individuals and groups rushing around from one ancient sacred site to another inserting crystals at them. To begin with, the stones of the sites are already crystals, erected by people with greater esoteric insight than any of the over-enthusiastic New Agers themselves. Further, if such activity really is a use of mysterious powers (highly debatable), then one person does not know what someone else may already have implanted at a site, and what 'vibrational interac-

PLATE 18   One of Harry Oldfield's crystal experiments used this model pyramid made of wood and copper layers, like a Wilhelm Reich orgone chamber. A crystal was placed on a sheet of film inside and left untouched in total darkness for 48 hours. After processing, the image in Plate 19 appeared on the film.

47

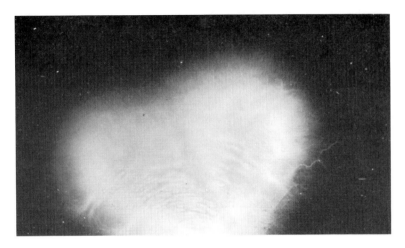

PLATE 19 This image was made without the application of light, electricity, or any other energy. The striated white 'haze' appeared where the crystal had been placed. Discharge paths like tiny bolts of lightning can be seen emerging from the white area [*Harry Oldfield*].

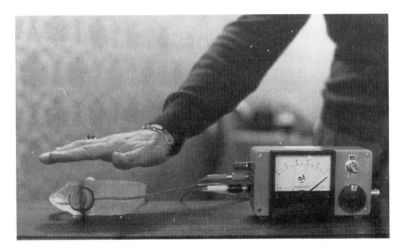

PLATE 20 In another early crystal experiment, Oldfield wired a quartz crystal to a high-impedence meter. After the meter needle had been at zero for a prolonged period, a woman sensitive mentally 'beamed' energy from her hand to the crystal. The needle moved to a full deflection across the meter (shown) as if the electrical status of the quartz had been somehow affected. The author, who could not cause the reaction himself, saw this experiment repeated several times, and on one occasion the effect was created by three sensitives at a distance of a metre or so .

tions' might thus be inadvertently triggered. And if these people really believe that Atlantis was brought to an end by the ignorant use of crystal energies, are they not in danger of repeating the self-same blunders? Even within the terms of its own belief system, the practice of planting crystals at ancient sites is indefensible.

THE DRAGON PROJECT

The concern with crystals at ancient places is just one aspect of the conviction held by many of those working outside the strict frame of archaeology that sacred sites possess or produce unusual energy effects. A rumour has been circulating for many years now that people can obtain shocks from standing stones similar to those caused by static electricity. There are specific accounts of this effect. Writing in 1974, Paul Screeton, journalist and former editor of *The Ley Hunter* magazine, recalled that from a stone at Hart, Cleveland, he 'and several others have felt a tingling sensation of varying intensity. My wife received an unpleasant shock when touching it one evening' (Screeton, 1974). Jack Roberts, who was a co-worker with Martin Brennan in the study of the action of sunlight and shadow on Neolithic chambered mounds in Ireland (Brennan, 1983), told me of a similar incident he experienced at Newgrange: he was entering the passage into the great mound one morning, and casually raised his hand to touch the lintel stone at the entrance as he passed underneath. He received a distinct shock that affected his whole arm. He gingerly reached out to the stone again, but this time nothing happened, as if the stone had 'discharged' itself. A retired military officer, and an active member of the National Trust, informed me of an occasion in 1974 when he received a shock off one of the Rollright circle stones which left his forearm numb for about 20 minutes afterwards. In 1979 a young volunteer site-warden at Rollright also told me, quite unprompted, that a stone in the ring had given him an 'electric shock'. I have heard such reports too often from too many people to dismiss the effect. It really does seem that some stones can on occasion store up an electrical charge in some way.

People have proceeded to make the wildest speculations regarding energy effects at prehistoric sites, however, and it has become difficult to sort the wheat from the chaff in such accounts. When I took over editorship of *The Ley Hunter* in 1976, it was simply *assumed* that energies existed at these places, both physical and 'spiritual' energies. The whole subject was confused, with statements of belief, pet theories, and speculation intermingling with purported actual experiences. I wanted to see what was actually *known*, so I invited articles for a special 'Earth

49

Energies Issue' of the magazine. The issue, no. 74, was duly published in the winter of 1976–7. While the articles were interesting, it was clear that no one had carried out accountable research into the nature or occurrence of supposed 'earth energies' at sites. There were theories, opinions, dowsing ideas, a couple of tentative suggestions for energy detection devices, and a few personal experiences. Over a period of months after this issue was published, I contacted various individuals whom I felt might have an interest in investigating possible energy effects at old stone monuments. I announced this process in *The Ley Hunter*, no. 78, later in 1977. Twenty people out of an invited 24 gathered at a London pub on 6 November 1977 to discuss the feasibility of setting up a research effort devoted to the study of possible site energies. Disciplines represented ranged through various aspects of physics, chemistry, electronics, dowsing, archaeology, and Earth Mysteries. At the meeting was the first scientist to have actually taken energy measurements (geomagnetic) at a standing stone—Dr Eduardo Balanovski (see Part Two).

Everyone agreed that it was desirable that such a research programme be set up, but there was considerable debate as to what form it should take. What energies should be monitored, and, at what levels of sensitivity? Where would the funding or the equipment come from? What sites would be used? There was also consideration whether psychic work should be part of the study as well as physical measurements. The questions and discussions went on for hours.

Gradually, the form of the project began to emerge. It was decided to run the effort as a two-pronged approach: a physical programme measuring known energies, and a 'psychic archaeology' programme using dowsers and various forms of psychics on site. Dr G.V. 'Don' Robins agreed to help co-ordinate the physical work (which he did up until 1982), and Californian researcher, John Steele, helped co-ordination of the psychic research (until 1986, when he had to return to the USA). I took on overall co-ordination and have continued to do so up to the time of writing.

Shortly after the November meeting, Robins, Steele, and I met to discuss details of co-ordination and to agree on a name for the project. After some discussion, Steele's suggestion of 'Dragon Project' was adopted, the dragon referring to one of the Feng shui symbols for an earth current.

Through the good offices of dowser Tom Graves, permission was obtained from the owner of the Rollright circle, Pauline Flick, to use the site as the project's main fieldbase. Rollright was a particularly suitable choice, as it has direct road access, is within 160 km (100 miles) of London, where most of the people involved in the project were then located, and it has a rich body of folklore attached to it, Moreover, in the fields around the circle were other, associated, megalithic sites.

In the following months, announcements appeared in *The Ley Hunter* about progress in getting the project into working shape, and appeals were made for donations of expertise and funds. Modest sums were promptly submitted by the magazine's readers, and electronic components for initial instrumentation were obtained, letterheads printed, and such field equipment as tents purchased.

The initial main problem was to determine the first work of the physical programme. While there was already a history of psychic and dowsing work at sites, there was none for physical measurements at such places, except for the work of Balanovski and Professor John Taylor at a stone near Crickhowell in South Wales (see Part Two). The possible range of physical monitoring was awesome, and clearly beyond the capacity of a small, volunteer outfit. The detailed study of any one aspect of the physical environment could swallow up the resources of a whole university department for years at a time. But it was also realized that we were dealing with virgin research territory, and that *anything* we managed to find out would be more than was currently known.

To target our inevitably limited research resources to the best advantage it was decided to take anecdotal material of energy effects at sites and to see what lines of enquiry they suggested for the physical-monitoring aspect of the project. The first area indicated in this way concerned ultrasound (high-frequency sound). This was prompted first of all by contact I had with a zoologist prior to the formation of the Dragon Project, who told me of a colleague of his who had been studying bat behaviour one night on a country estate. At dawn he was returning to his base with his 'bat detector' (a wide-band ultrasonic receiver capable of detecting high-frequency sound emitted by bats) still switched on. As he passed an ancient site on the estate, he noticed the receiver was registering a signal for which he could find no obvious cause.

The zoologist passed the anecdote on to me for what it was worth, in case it fitted into any of our Earth Mysteries enquiries. This was later augmented by archaeologist John Barnatt, who, while engaged on surveying the henge of Arbor Low in Derbyshire, was interrupted by a man who wandered onto the site. He asked Barnatt if he knew why the skylarks frequented Arbor Low. On admitting that he had no idea, Barnatt was informed by the gentleman that it was due to the ultrasound being emitted by the site's recumbent stones! Although slender, such leads were felt by the project co-ordinators to be sufficient to warrant the construction of a wide-band ultrasonic receiver of the 'bat-detector' type.

In October 1978, John Barnatt produced a survey of the Rollright circle for the project. He also probed the bases of the stones so that we would have an idea of which ones in the ring were most likely to be original. Also by this time, the first ultrasonic receiver was ready for use. It was decided that Robins should be first into the field with the instrument, thus opening the fieldwork phase of the project. Robins arrived at the Rollright Stones before dawn on 21 October. To everyone's frank surprise, he did obtain anomalous pulses on the machine's dial over the period of sunrise. Accounts of this work and other aspects of the physical programme are given in Part Two.

As the fieldwork commenced, the project's geological consultant, Paul McCartney, began to study a claim made by John Michell in 1969 that megalithic sites were located close to geological faults. Faults are cracks or fissures in the earth's crust, and often create localized regions of disturbed electromagnetic energy within the landscape. They are also typical features in the kind of terrain that harbours unusual light phenomena, as we learn later. McCartney's research was able to confirm Michell's informal observation as far as stone circles are concerned. Rollright, too, fitted the pattern: the circle is indeed only a field away from an isolated local fault.

Core personnel on the Dragon Project increased with the addition of Roy Cooper, a surveyor attached to Oxford University, and born and bred in the county. He became the local anchor-man at Rollright and has shouldered a great deal of project work. In due course we were also joined by Rodney Hale, an experienced electronics engineer with his own electronics design company. Around the basic team, many experts and general helpers came and went over the months and years. Many sites other than Rollright have been visited by the Dragon Project, but the Oxfordshire circle has remained the main reference location for the effort.

Dowsers and psychics also began to be attracted to the project and Steele got the psychic programme into action. Areas of monitoring lying between the physical and psychic spheres were introduced, such as Kirlian electrophotography techniques and audio recording of 'electronic-voice phenomena', in which apparently paranormal voices are found lodged in the background hiss of specialized tape recordings. Slightly more substantial funding was obtained from the Threshold Foundation UK, and a few hundred additional pounds were donated by the British Society of Dowsers and a handful of individuals. It was not a great deal, but it allowed the project to proceed in its own modest way, and for a co-ordinating office to be set up.

Over 1983 and 1984, the Dragon Project joined with the Association for the Scientific Study of Anomalous Phenomena (ASSAP) to conduct the 'Gaia Programme', in which thirty sites, along with control locations stretching from Scotland to Cornwall, were subjected to radiation monitoring. Scores of volunteers living throughout the country were involved, and many sites that had not previously been looked at by the

PLATE 21 Trained geochemist, Paul McCartney, looks south from the King's Men circle towards the Rollright fault. On one occasion the stone behind him reportedly gave a volunteer site-warden a shock like static electricity.

Dragon Project were monitored, albeit in a necessarily brief, 'one-off' manner. Geiger counters were sent by post from one regional group of monitors to another. The operation proceeded smoothly, except for an incident in which one of the instruments managed to switch itself on during postal sorting at Oxford. The bleeping package created a bomb scare that caused the evacuation of the building! Some findings of the Gaia Programme are included in later parts of this book.

As the work of the Dragon Project developed and became more widely known, we found ourselves inadvertently becoming the source of modern folklore. Journalists visited Rollright during project sessions, and distorted stories got out into the Press on some occasions, while anti-technology 'New Agers' felt the use of electric instrumentation at a site was tantamount to sacrilege. Some people seemed to imagine that a geiger counter was actually *producing* radiation instead of merely listening to the chatter of a primordial natural force. Extreme rumours circulated saying that John Steele was a CIA agent, and that a project monitor had died from unspecified energy effects at Rollright! Fortunately, much of this silliness has now subsided, and the project is widely accepted as a non-intrusive, multi-disciplinary, and multi-mode way of trying to understand the enigmatic stone monuments of prehistory.

The Dragon Project has been a shoestring operation, conducted fitfully over the years by a largely changing team of people. Its main achievements have been to bring people of various disciplines and outlooks together, and to start clearing the ground around the whole issue of possible unusual energetic effects at ancient sites. It has been able to point to some interesting site anomalies worthy of further study in radiation, magnetism, apparent ultrasound, radio propagation, infra-red photography, and other areas. With this 'clearing operation' more or less fulfilled, the project became The Dragon Project Trust in 1988 in the hope of attracting more substantial funding, enabling it to concentrate on certain areas of research in a more thorough manner. This phase awaits commencement at the time of writing. For details of the trust see page 217.

Over approximately the same period as the early parts of the Dragon Project (and unknown to either party), Belgian researcher Pierre Méreaux was conducting similar enquiries at the huge megalithic complex around Carnac in Brittany. Some of his findings will also be discussed in later pages.

So—the rumours of power places persist: from the record and traditions of ancient peoples and societies, from folklore, from personal experiences, and, now, from measurable, scientific work. The human race up until our own times has accepted the existence of some all-pervading universal energy, an energy that flows through the land as well as objects and living things. It will be a long while until our own science can return to that viewpoint, and it is beyond the brief of this present book to explore the nature of this subtle energy, this *ch'i*. But what we can do now for the first time is to look at specific sites in Britain (and in Part Three also elsewhere in the world) where certain objective energy effects have been measured or reliably observed and attempt to assess their significance. In some cases the reader will be able to confirm directly energy effects for the modest cost of a liquid-filled compass.

The forces current research has so far disclosed at the sacred places may only rarely be exotic, but we will see that even such known energies as radiation and magnetism can tell us previously unknown things about particular sites and possibly reveal secrets of their ritual use and the knowledge of their builders. The ancient sites are places of learning; repositories of knowledge about former understandings of our planet and our relationship with it.

It is time now to go to school.

PART TWO

ON THE GROUND:
THE SITES

3 INTRODUCTION

The study of noteworthy energy effects at prehistoric sites is in a state similar to that of aeronautics in 1904: there have been a few string-and-sealing-wax trials, but many more experiments with hot air. A mere beginning has been made on a formidable task, and that is why we refer in this section to only a few dozen out of all the prehistoric sites there are to be found in Britain.

Even Rollright, field home of the Dragon Project, has by no means had a thorough study of its geophysical properties, though more energy-oriented work has been done there than at any other single site. Energy findings at other monuments have resulted, variously, from chance observations to planned sessions of several hours' monitoring. *No site in Britain has been fully checked for energy anomalies.* Sites really need to be monitored continuously for radiation, magnetism, ultrasound, and other energies for months or years at a stretch, but resources simply do not exist for such unorthodox work to be carried out at this level. All we can do in this book is to look at a representative selection of what has so far been measured or observed.

Energy information on the sites included in this section comes from the findings of the Dragon Project or the Gaia Programme, from other work or observations by independent individuals, and from 1988 research carried out by myself specifically for this book. I am deliberately selecting information on objective effects, leaving out nearly all dowsing and psychic references to energies as they are contentious areas on their own and are not the concern of this particular enquiry. A few paranormal and dowsing experiences are included, however, where these may have a possible bearing on geophysical conditions.

Knowledge of transient phenomena, or phenomena that has only just begun to be noticed, of necessity relies on chance human observation. Some types of energy effects are, therefore, recorded here anecdotally. There is no way of avoiding this if the record is to be maintained. But the cases I have included are based on what I am satisfied are reliable accounts. Others I am less confident about I have omitted and, of course, I have no doubt people have had numerous other experiences that have not come to my notice.

While the Rollright Stones have been used to test a wide variety of monitoring approaches—some of them employed only once or twice—the principal areas of physical research there, and almost exclusively at other sites, have been to do with magnetism, radiation, light phenomena, and, possibly, ultrasonic emissions. Most sites, in fact, have had preliminary checks for only one or two of these. It is just a beginning, but a start that has had to have been made: pet theories or effortless speculations really will not do any longer—the era of the hot-air experiments now needs to draw to a close. Longer-term and more detailed research can be based on the indications revealed in this section for those who really want to learn from the sites and not merely project their beliefs onto them.

Of the four main areas of energy effect referred to above, only the light phenomena are likely to relate to an unknown, exotic energy. The others are well known to science, and might seem somewhat mundane to fans of such movies as *Raiders of the Lost Ark* or *Romancing the Stone*. There is nothing paranormal about these forces, but we are looking at them in a context not studied by orthodox science, and it is that context that is important and that holds the promise of revealing what may have been a prehistoric knowledge and usage of the effects of natural energies. Whether scientist or layperson, I feel all those of us who have been engaged in the search for unusual forces at sites—and I very much include myself here—have been too concerned to find some fabulous, world-shattering new energy effect to see what is really at the sites in energy terms. We have been looking for something out of science fiction rather than out of prehistory. The mitigating factor is, though, that archaeologists have not even been looking. Between all of us, alternative and orthodox researchers alike, the presence and actual nature of site energies have slipped by unobserved.

I hope by the end of this book I will have persuaded at least some readers that the energy effects we can really find at these old, mysterious places are as remarkable as any toy-town notion we might have invented, and come out of the megalith builders' deep, intimate knowledge of their materials and environment and the relationship their minds and bodies had with them. In other words, the physics of shamanism that belonged to the world of thousands of years ago, not to the fantasies of the late twentieth century.

While the secular cult of contemporary academic research seems unable to appreciate properly the over-riding importance altered states of consciousness and the reality of the spirit world had in prehistory, a technology was nevertheless built up around those needs; a technology that has its own archaeology if we have the wit to identify it. It is an area of ancient life that need not be dismissed to some shadowy region of 'ritual' or 'religious belief' beyond the brief of the archaeologist. To some extent, the sites can still tell us something about it.

Before going on to describe specific sites, it will be helpful to consider basic background information on each of the four main types of energy.

RADIATION

It is difficult nowadays to talk about nuclear radiation without images of Hiroshima, Chernobyl, Three Mile Island, or Sellafield being conjured before the mind's eye. But these producers and users of ionizing radiation are purely artificial, technological phenomena, involving dosages not normally encountered in Nature—not earthbound Nature at any rate. It is not these high levels of radiation that concern us here.

Radioactive decay involves alpha and beta particles and gamma-rays. Natural radiation has always existed throughout the universe; it is part of the network of forces that sustain it. It is one of the breaths of God. Natural radiation is not different from artificially produced radiation except in terms of its source and the concentrations in which it occurs. Natural radioactivity pervades the whole environment and is usually the major source of radiation most people are exposed to. Beyond certain levels radiation is, as we know, harmful to human beings and other living things, causing malignant diseases and other complications. The levels ('dose') that are considered safe or acceptable are subject to social and political expedients, and vary from one society to another, and from time to time.

Natural radioactivity in our environment comes from both terrestrial and astronomical sources. Cosmic rays constantly bombard our atmosphere from deep interstellar space and from the sun. These interact with molecules in the upper atmosphere causing secondary particles. Radiation dose increases with altitude and also with latitude, because more cosmic rays enter near the poles than the equator.

Numerous components of the earth's crust are radioactive to some extent, and particularly radioactive material, such as uranium, thorium, and potassium-40, are dispersed through soil and rock in various low concentrations. One of the decay products of uranium is the radioactive gas, *radon* (radon-222), which can emerge from the ground into the atmosphere where it continues to decay. Gamma-rays are emitted by the radioactive materials in the ground and, of course, from building materials extracted from the earth. The igneous rock, granite, is particularly radioactive, and areas where granite outcrops extensively, or where large amounts of the stone are used as a building material in urban areas (Aberdeen, Scotland, for example), will have higher background radiation counts than places with less granite. This factor, as we shall see, may have been deliberately exploited by megalith builders where the opportunity presented itself.

It is estimated by the National Radiological Protection Board (NRPB) in the UK that in the average annual radiation dose received by the population, gamma-rays account for 16 per cent of the total dose, cosmic rays for 13 per cent, and radon for 33 per cent. While the overall nature of ionizing radiation is well understood by science, there is less known about its behaviour at intimate levels within the landscape. While I will be showing that concentrations of natural radioactivity at doses equivalent to high background levels might be responsible for subtle but important effects on human consciousness, as well as a curious physical phenomenon, the official attitude would be that such levels could have no effects at all. In my opinion this view obtains only because the energy in its natural habitat has not been studied sufficiently closely. Orthodox science has always under-estimated how sensitive living creatures can be to low-level energy in the environment (see Part Three).

Indeed, the official monitoring of gamma-ray dose out of doors only began in Britain as recently as 1980, and even then was carried on as incidental to other NRPB work. This was two years after the commencement of fieldwork on the Dragon Project, where we had to try to work out how genuine radiation anomalies at sites might be identified. The project had to take many thousands of geiger counter readings overall in order to be able to determine what an unusual high or low radiation count would be at any given site compared with its regional environment.

The aim of the NRPB readings was to take at least one measurement in every 10 km^2 of the Ordnance Survey grid. While this gives an overall picture of regional variations in gamma radiation throughout the British Isles, it does not address the more detailed variations unorthodox energy research at ancient sites needs to study.

Interest in levels of outdoor, landscape radiation has been given a boost in recent years due to the concern about radon gas building up in homes, and the Chernobyl disaster. The incidence of radon-gas emission is highest in granitic areas, and it has come to be realised that it presents a health threat to people in such areas, particularly those who live in well-sealed homes. Radon can creep up through the ground and into buildings through foundation defects, pipes, and other points of access and then be sucked into the lower-pressure house environment. The gas, instead of dispersing naturally as it does in the open air, increases its concentrations in such dwellings. As it decays in the air, the gas produces solid radionuclides—'radon daughters'—that attach themselves to dust particles and can be inhaled. It is believed that long exposure to this can increase the risk of lung cancer. Thousands of people in Sweden, Britain, the USA, and other countries have now been monitored to test population exposure to radon. In Britain, the worst-affected county is Cornwall, which has extensive areas underlain by a huge granite intrusion. Interestingly, Cornwall also has one of the highest—if not *the* highest—concentrations of megaliths in Britain, as well as a particular type of prehistoric underground chamber known as a fogou, which we will find yields some vital clues about the use of natural energies in prehistory.

Thousands of dwellings in Britain alone, especially in Cornwall and Devon, are affected by high levels of radon, and the matter has been the subject of debate in Parliament. In effect, such debates are dealing with geomancy (we can be sure, for instance, that radon was one aspect of the noxious *sha* that the Feng shui geomant strove to avoid when siting buildings). The lesson of the continuing study of radon in dwellings is that failure to take geomantic factors into account can be expensive in terms of money and resources, and can be potentially damaging to health. It has been estimated that in perhaps as many as eight million homes in the USA, radon levels may exceed currently established safety levels.

Radiation can be detected by certain types of photographic emulsion, by geiger tubes, and by scintillation counters. I also suspect that living organisms can directly sense the presence of increased radioactivity (see Part Three). The radiation information at sites referred to in this section has been obtained through numerous pieces of instrumentation, ranging from very basic geiger counters giving beeps that had to be manually counted, to more sophisticated radiation monitors and scintillometers. An experimental multi-tubed geiger counter, designed by Melford Designs Ltd of St Albans, was also employed in some of the 1988 research. In some cases, findings have been cross-checked with different models of geiger counter.

These detectors record essentially random events, and averages of their readings have to be used to give meaningful information. Therefore geiger counter readings have been taken at sites and in their environments for precisely timed periods of minutes or hours, then averaged to *counts per minute*. Certain set procedures were adopted during Dragon Project and Gaia Programme work in the monitoring of sites, their local backgrounds, and selected non-megalithic control sites. Counts per minute (cpm) can theoretically be converted to specific units of radiation measurement, but the energy work at sites has proceeded with cpm, and consists mainly of comparing sites and parts of sites with background measurements, and in some cases with readings taken elsewhere. Due to this, and because the various instruments involved have inevitably used their own count rates, I usually give radiation indications at sites in the following guide in terms of factors or percentages relative to background or other selected measurements.

MAGNETISM

The earth, like other planetary bodies, has a magnetic field—the geomagnetic field. It permeates the earth's body and atmosphere and extends thousands of miles into space. How it is produced is not exactly understood by scientists, but the general current hypothesis is that motions in the earth's core (probably consisting of a solid iron-rich alloy inner core and fluid outer core of molten iron sulphide) caused by a mix of possible stimuli, such as the earth's rotation, currents caused by heat transference between the liquid core and the surrounding mantle, and the exchange of energy between the slowly circulating mantle and the core, all act something like a dynamo producing accompanying magnetic fields. The earth as a whole acts like one giant magnet, but its magnetic poles do not coincide precisely with the rotational poles—in fact, they migrate considerably over periods of time. So 'magnetic north'—that area to which a compass needle points in the northern hemisphere—will almost always be different from true north or the grid north of map.

The geomagnetic field does not simply lie over the land like a sheet on a bed: since it is approximately dipolar, the magnetic field lines at the earth's surface are inclined at an angle that increases with latitude. In Britain, this angle is between 60 and 70 degrees. In the northern hemisphere the field is inclined downwards, pointing straight down at the north magnetic pole. In the southern hemisphere the field is inclined upwards, also at an angle increasing with latitude, pointing straight up at the south magnetic pole. Only at the geomagnetic equator is the field horizontal.

Components of the geomagnetic field are subject to diurnal (daily) variations—particularly because of solar action on the electrical properties of the atmosphere. The local field in a given area can also be subjected to movement due to various stimuli.

Many kinds of rock contain sufficient quantities of such iron-bearing minerals as magnetite (lodestone) to display a measurable magnetization *induced* in them by the earth's present-day magnetic field. Common igneous rocks, such as basalt or granite, tend to show considerably higher magnetic susceptibilities than sedimentary rocks.

But this induced magnetization may be only part of the total magnetism trapped in the rock. (Basalts, for instance, are significantly magnetic in their own right.) When iron minerals solidify from the molten magma they become magnetized when the rock cools beneath a certain critical temperature known as the Curie Point. This 'fossil' or *remanent* magnetization provides a unique finger-print of the magnetic fields of past geological ages. It sometimes bears little relationship to the induced magnetization (such are the idiosyncrasies of the earth's ever-changing field) and, indeed, it is not uncommonly the stronger component of the total magnetism measured in the rock. Rocks with such complex magnetic histories can cause quite startling effects on compasses, and we will see how these more dramatic examples of 'magnetic stones' can sometimes be found occurring naturally at places that have been identified as sacred, or actually incorporated into megalithic structures.

By looking back at the magnetic record held in stone, geologists have been able to learn that the magnetic poles of our planet have reversed themselves at various irregular intervals every 100,000 years or so. The cause and implications of such pole reversals are not clearly understood at present.

Units for various types of magnetic measurement include the oersted, gauss, gamma, and tesla. The earth's field averages around 0.4 gauss. In Britain the field is about 0.47 gauss or 47,000 nT (nano-tesla—*nano* means 10^{-9} of a unit).

The first instrument used for detecting the magnetic field was the lodestone—a shaped piece of the strongly magnetic mineral magnetite. The modern instruments usually used to measure the magnitude or direction of the geomagnetic field are magnetometers. These come in a wide range of sensitivities and work to various principles. The two instruments owned by the Dragon Project, for instance, are of what is called the 'flux-gate' type, and have a sensitivity down to around 15 nT and respond to movements in the magnetic field as well as field strength. As will be described, unexplained variations of low-level magnetism within standing stones have been measured, both by the project's magnetometers and other instrumentation. The trouble with measuring at these low levels, however, is that all kinds of ambient variables in the environment can affect readings, and have to be carefully guarded against. It was the Carn Ingli case (site 13 in the following guide) that alerted us to the fact that some magnetic effects at prehistoric places were of a kind able to register unambiguously on simple magnetic compasses, and that we need not always have to use magnetometers.

Orthodox archaeology also uses magnetometers. Their function in this context is to locate areas of magnetic disturbance caused by the burial of iron objects, places such as kilns or hearths where there has been intense heat and burning, or disturbed topsoil such as infilled pits and ditches (topsoil is apparently more magnetic than subsoil). In this way, a site being considered for excavation can be plotted for points of interest without the ground being physically disturbed, thus targeting future excavational activity more accurately.

As will be seen in Part Three, it is certain that many living organisms can sense variations in the geomagnetic field directly, and it is highly probable that human beings have such sensitivity as well.

PLATE 22   Dragon Project magnetometers monitoring the Whispering Knights, Rollright.

ULTRASOUND

Ultrasound, like all sound, is a pressure wave in the air. It is called 'ultra' because it is at frequencies higher than those used by human hearing, the upper limit of which is usually around 20 kiloHertz (kHz or KHz—one kHz is a thousand cycles per second). Numerous other creatures can produce or hear into ultrasonic frequencies—a dog-whistle, for instance, produces an ultrasonic signal virtually soundless to the human ear, yet will be readily distinguished by canine hearing. The two supreme mammalian masters of ultrasound, however, are bats and dolphins. Bats emit ultrasonic squeaks for echo-location purposes, their specially adapted ears picking up the echo from objects in the environment. Dolphins probably use ultrasound for a variety of purposes, certainly for echo-location used in hunting and possibly even for communication amongst themselves. A dolphin has a dome-shaped structure on its head that actually focuses the bursts of mixed-frequency sounds emitted by the creature's larynx. Both bats and dolphins sometimes produce ultrasonic frequencies reaching up to 200 kHz.

Apart from these living sources, there is not much else in nature that produces ultrasound. Friction tends to produce an ultrasonic component, however, and so wind blowing through leaves and grass can produce a very low-level background ultrasonic signal, and it is pos-

PLATE 23 The remarkable and mysterious dolphin makes use of ultrasound, which is focused by the protuberance on its head.

sible that some types of geological friction may also produce both ultrasound and infrasound (very low-frequency sound). Artificially generated ultrasound has a number of uses in science and commerce, including certain healing applications. While most people cannot consciously hear above 20 kHz, there is some preliminary German research that indicates humans can be subliminally aware of much higher frequencies of sound.

The Dragon Project has had the use of a number of different ultrasonic receivers, some wide-band (ranging from low kHz frequencies to around 100 kHz), narrow-band machines cut at specific frequencies (such as 40 kHz), and various designs giving either meter or audio output. The anomalous effects undoubtedly displayed by some of these machines at various times during Dragon Project work have not yet been definitely confirmed as resulting from ultrasonic signals: this has been simply an assumption as they have been picked up only on receivers designed for ultrasound detection, the transducers of which are supposed to be screened against other interference. Nevertheless, the occurrence of ultrasound is so odd at a place like a stone circle that debate still circulates as to whether some as yet unidentified spurious effect is involved. Actual findings with ultrasound detectors are described below, along with the qualifications we have to bear in mind with regard to those findings.

LIGHT PHENOMENA

There is powerful evidence to suggest that our planet can produce a curious form of lightball energy at certain times in particular types of terrain. I have called these phenomena 'earth lights'. This is not the place to examine the mighty body of evidence telling of their actuality—that has been well established elsewhere (see, for example, Persinger, 1977; Devereux, 1982; Tributsch, 1982; Devereux, McCartney, and Robins, 1983; Devereux, 1989).

We know that lights can be produced during earthquake activity ('earthquake lights') and accompanying powerful electrical storms ('ball lightning'). But similar lights are also seen without either of these conditions being present. They usually haunt specific locales, either intensively for periods of weeks, months, or even a few years, or else sporadically over decades or centuries. My own research has led me to believe that these lights are popping out of the earth's crust somewhere or other all the time. The lights definitely have a *geography*. In the past these things have been seen as dragons, fairies, omens, curious types of 'meteor', unfamiliar terrestrial technology (usually that of an enemy during wartime), and now as alien spacecraft. Rarely are they per-

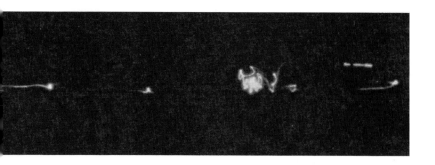

PLATE 24 Dancing lights over the prairie near Marfa, Texas, leave trails on this photograph by James Crocker. Such lights have been reported from the area for over 100 years. Earth lights tend to haunt fairly localized geographical areas [*James Crocker*].

ceived for what they are—an extraordinary natural phenomenon belonging to this planet. These lights usually measure 50 cm (1–2 ft) across, but smaller and larger examples have been reported.

Investigators believe these earth lights arise as a result of a mix of geological and terrestrial electromagnetic factors, with the main 'motor' probably being low-level stress in the earth's crust, below the threshold required for a noticeable tremor, especially along fault lines where tectonic movement is most likely to occur and where there are sometimes mineral deposits that may affect the electromagnetic conditions of the area. (It is certainly the case that medieval miners of tin and copper used to look for the issue of lights from the ground to help them locate rich mineral veins.)

It is in precisely this kind of geological country where most stone circles are located. Critics have dismissed the proximity of such sites to faulting and other areas of geological disturbance as a purely fortuitous connection coming about simply because these are areas where the megalith builders found ready supplies of stone. I have argued (Devereux, 1982), that the more likely incidence of light phenomena in these regions could also have been a (shamanistic) factor in the siting of certain monuments, and I return to this theme in Part Three, where examples of the conscious use of faulting for ancient siting purposes will be given. And later in this section it will be shown that light phenomena are still reported at certain sites.

Although geological and electromagnetic factors are very likely to be involved with the production of the lights, the exact mechanism of their manifestation is not yet understood, and the energy involved is exotic. It is either an unfamiliar form of electromagnetism or some as yet unidentified energy altogether. It seems to flicker in and out, as it were, on the very edge of physical manifestation, and may have revolutionary properties. It may, for example, be related to consciousness itself, if we can allow ourselves to picture consciousness as a field effect rather than some type of skull-centred transient phenomenon. The lights may be the closest we can come to seeing the Chinese *ch'i* or all those other names the subtle force goes under.

These, then, are the principal manifestations we will be noting at the sites included here, though there will be a few other less explored ones that will be dealt with as they arise. As Dragon Project fieldbase, the Rollright complex has seen more experimental efforts of the fledgling field of unorthodox site-energy research than any other ancient monument on earth, and while most of that work has produced results that remain inconclusive, there have been a few real insights granted by the Rollright Stones that point to important areas of future enquiry. For this reason, I give the site pride of place, dealing with it separately to the range of other places described in the main guide to sites later in this section.

4 THE ROLLRIGHT STONES

This complex lies alongside a country road linking the A44 and A34, about 5 km (3 miles) north-west of Chipping Norton, itself approximately 29 km (18 miles) north-west of Oxford, and can be located at grid reference SP 296308 on the Ordnance Survey 1:50 000 sheet 151. The Cross Hands Inn stands at the junction of the country road with the A44. The stones consist of a circle, 'The King's Men', to the south of the country road; a lone monolith, the 'King Stone', to its north, and the 'Whispering Knights'—a collapsed dolmen—in a field about 400 m (1/4 mile) east-south-east of the circle.

The country road runs along a ridge and is, indeed, the ancient Cotswold ridgeway, part of the Jurassic Way. It defines a county

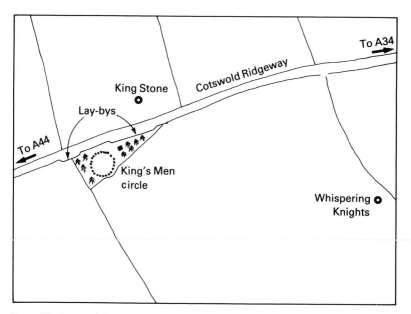

FIG. 6 The layout of the Rollright Stones.

PLATE 25   Northern part of the King's Men circle, Rollright.

boundary where it runs past the circle, so the King Stone is, in fact, in Warwickshire with the rest of the complex in Oxfordshire. Other megalithic remains once existed within the general vicinity of the Rollright Stones, and there was also a scattering of burial mounds or barrows in the area, though little remains of these. Recent archaeological work shows the immediate area to have been a focus for human activity from the late Mesolithic ('Middle Stone' Age) period (fifth millennium BC and earlier) through the Neolithic and Bronze Ages and into Roman and Anglo-Saxon times (Lambrick, 1983)

The King's Men is almost a true circle, approximately 31.6 m (104 ft) in diameter, consisting of gnarled and holed limestone blocks, most of them only metre or so high. The tallest stone reaches to over 2.3 m (7 ft). The circle has not been dated, but large circular rings of this type are now thought to date to the third millennium BC. The Whispering Knights may be older. The King Stone is almost 2.4 m (8 ft) tall.

Leslie Grinsell comments (1976) that the Rollright Stones have 'one of the richest collections of folklore of any British prehistoric site'. The main theme associated with the stones is that of petrifaction: a king and his men were accosted by a witch who challenged the regent to see if he could see the village of Long Compton beyond the next ridge in seven king-sized strides. He tried but failed, as a mound rose up magically to block his view on his seventh long stride. He was turned to stone by the witch as were his knights (the dolmen) and his army (the stone circle). The witch turned herself into 'an eldern tree'. In earlier centuries it was the custom for local villagers to stand in a circle around the stone on Midsummer Eve. The elder—no one now seems sure of its location—was cut and if it bled 'the King moved his head'. The ridge that does indeed block the view of Long Compton from the position of the King Stone was always assumed to be natural, but excavations in recent years have shown that it is, in fact, partially artificial, with a cairn having been placed on the natural rise of the ground, and a round barrow having been at its western end. Neolithic or Bronze Age cremation remains were found on top and beside the cairn site.

Other folk stories state that the stones used to go down to a brook on New Year's Eve to drink at midnight, but now they do so when they hear the Long Compton clock strike midnight; bad luck has attended those who have tried to move the stones, and stones moved from the site return more easily than they were taken; the king and his men will return to life at an hour of great need for the country, and the stones of the circle cannot be counted. This last theme has some foundation in fact, as the number of stones (presently over 70) has varied in different surveys and drawings over the last few centuries. This can partially be

FIG. 7 An old lithograph showing a view from the Whispering Knights towards the King's Men.

71

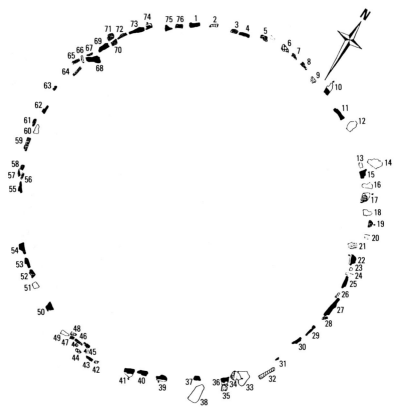

FIG. 8 John Barnatt's 1978 survey of the Rollright circle. The blacked-in stones are those most likely to have been original, and those in tone are possibly original [*John Barnatt*].

put down to the fact that pieces of broken stones fell to the ground along the circumference of the circle, and came to be counted in with the originals—not as improbable as it sounds, because many of the King's Men stones are small. It seems that around 23 of the present stones in the ring may have been original.

Specific traditions became attached to the King Stone. For centuries pieces of the stone were chipped away for good luck, accounting for the big 'bite' out of its eastern side. The monolith was also said to promote fertility, and young women used to go to it at night and touch it with their breasts. The fairies traditionally dance around the stone at night, coming out of a hole in the ground nearby. (On one occasion a Dragon Project monitor, working in misty pre-dawn hours at the King Stone, got the fright of his life when he saw shadowy figures passing near the

PLATE 26 The strangely shaped King Stone, Rollright.

monolith. Summoning up his courage, he approached the beings to find they were in fact soldiers on a training exercise making for the Royal Observer Corps bunker in the King Stone field!)

Perhaps because it was called 'whispering', or perhaps for more objective reasons, the Whispering Knights dolmen was used up until as recently as the nineteenth century by girls and young women as an oracle. They would put their ears to a hollow in the stones, or even climb up onto them, in order to hear the megaliths whisper answers to their questions. It might not be entirely without relevance to this tradition that around 9.15 pm on 1 March 1980, four persons engaged on round-the-clock monitoring work for the Dragon Project heard 'very pronounced' ticking noises emerging from the vicinity of the Whispering Knights, along with a humming sound. This was precisely at the time of the full moon. The ticking sound was also heard close to the King Stone, but less loudly.

There seems to have been a local tradition up until the early years of this century at least, that light phenomena could be seen at the

PLATE 27 The collapsed dolmen known as the Whispering Knights, Rollright.

PLATE 28 Southern part of King's Men circle, with Whispering Knights in the distance across the field.

Rollright Stones, as the late Mrs L. Chapman recorded in *The Ley Hunter* (1982):

> In 1919 I was sent to work in Warwickshire and lodged at Long Compton—near the Rollright Stones. I was curious about the stones and wished to go and inspect them but my landlady was afraid to go as lights had been seen and there were tales of people losing their memory after touching them. I thought it was just village gossip and decided to go by myself. I went one evening after work and was fingering one of the group of 'Whispering Knights'... when my hand and arm began to tingle badly and I felt as though I was being pushed away... The tingling in my hand and arm lasted throughout the night and the next day.

Strange lights at sites meant only one thing as far as the rural mind was concerned—*fairies*, hence the fear associated with such reports. No Dragon Project monitors staying overnight at the circle have reported any light phenomena, but a friend of co-ordinator John Steele who stayed at the circle for a two-week period in August 1980 (a longer period than experienced by most people), claimed that

> for several nights when there was no moon, I saw a pool of diffuse white light which seemed to be coming out of the ground; it rose a bit above the stones and then tapered off. The whole centre of the circle was generating light.

> (Steele, 1982)

It is of course noteworthy that Chapman gives yet another account of a shock received from a standing stone (see Part One).

The King's Men circle has certainly been subject to the attentions of those engaged in witchcraft from at least Tudor times. Genuine Wicca is of course a harmless and excellent religious persuasion, but the stones have also been subject to less savoury ritualists. People staying overnight near the circle on separate occasions have witnessed bizarre ceremonies, certainly not Wiccan, and in the 1970s some appalling group ritually killed a spaniel, leaving its remains in the circle. It was this outrage, coupled with general hooliganism at the circle, that made the owner, Pauline Flick, decide to fence the site off from the road and install a custodian's hut in the grove of trees adjacent to the circle. Occasional hooligan attacks take place even now, but the worst excesses seem to have abated.

My first visit to the site, in the last rays of sunlight on 3 July 1971, underlines the ritual attraction the circle seems to possess. As my colleagues and I drove up to the circle, which at that time was open to the road, we could see a man and woman dancing within it. One of the people in our car was a practising cabbalist, and he led the way from the vehicle to the circle. As he entered the ring of stones he turned on his heel with such suddenness I stopped dead in my tracks at the perimeter of the circle. The two dancers had scurried to the far side of the site, while the cabbalist fixed his eyes on a third person sitting crossed-legged against the tallest stone in the ring. The two men locked into what I can only describe as a battle of wills—the sense of energy within the circle was almost palpable. Eventually, the seated man rose and backed out of the circle. The two dancers joined him and all three moved slowly away along the road in the direction of the A34. When we returned to our rental car after exploring the site, the key would not turn in the ignition, though the vehicle had been working perfectly all day. The cabbalist advised leaving it for 20 minutes or so. We did, and the key then turned with ease.

A rarely mentioned local tradition that I have heard of associated with the site is that the stones can emit a sound at twilight. This is of potential interest because of the possible ultrasound emissions the Dragon Project may have detected at the stones. In Part One it was mentioned that the first ultrasonic monitoring at the site began in October 1978. As statements regarding the ultrasound research have been published widely elsewhere (Robins, 1980, 1982, 1985; numerous media reports by Dragon Project spokespersons), causing it to become the most known aspect of the project, it is important I give the more complete account here, so the reader can properly assess the problems the findings at Rollright present and at the same time get a glimpse into the difficult nature of poorly funded, unorthodox energy research at sites. (The first, tentative findings we announced became so garbled that when I was interviewed for a cable TV show in New York in 1980, the interviewer asked me, 'What about the sounds you have been recording at Stonehenge?'—a misunderstanding he had picked up from an Australian newspaper article!)

THE ULTRASOUND RIDDLE

Readings taken during the October session and on subsequent occasions through the autumn, until curtailed by the harsh winter, showed an apparent ultrasonic pulsing over the dawn period in the immediate area of the King Stone but not at the circle. The wide-band ultrasound receiver used for these early experiments gave a readout on a dial gauged from 0 to 10. Background ultrasound was very slight and registered if at all only as a random, slight shivering of the needle. When the unusual signal was present, the needle would move in distinct, purposeful two-second pulses to between 2 and 4 on the meter scale. At a monitoring session in December, Don Robins and I noted a curious phenomenon that was never repeated: inside the circle we

PLATE 29 The Dragon Project's first
ultrasound receiver.

PLATE 29 The Dragon Project's first
ultrasound receiver.

could not obtain even the background flutter of readings. We repeatedly (five times) moved inside and outside the ring of stones. Each time
the flicker would pick up outside the circle, but completely cease
within. No explanation of this—which Robins dignified with the term
'zero-field effect'—was ever forthcoming.

As the winter weather abated in February 1979, ultrasonic monitoring was once more continued. This time, readings on the receiver
showed full-scale deflections and were obtained at all points in the
Rollright complex, including the roadway between the King Stone and
the circle, and positions quite distant in the countryside around the
stones. Subsequent readings taken at the site through the spring
showed the pulsing activity, but its intensity generally declined, and
the tremendous February outburst was not repeated again. Over the
summer months virtually no activity was recorded at all.

It so happened that some of the active ultrasonic monitoring sessions
between November 1978 and April 1979 closely coincided with full- or
new-moon periods. For the times this happened a distinct pattern was
noted: the pulsing effect would start 8 to 10 minutes before sunrise at
new moon, and 25 to 35 minutes before sunrise at full moon. This
pattern was startling, with only one slight discrepancy in seven instances, but it proved logistically impossible within the limitations of the
project's resources of time and personnel to synchronize sufficient
further monitoring sessions with lunar phase. So a statistical confirma-
tion of this potential pattern was not obtained. On all occasions when
apparent ultrasound was being recorded, the pulsing would continue
through sunrise and continue up to two or three hours afterwards,
when the random background flutter of the needle would be re-

established. Checks with the instrument during later periods of the day never resulted in the appearance of the pulsing pattern. Sunset monitoring rarely revealed any activity, and when it did occur it would be just a few swift 'spikes' of activity on the receiver's dial. This occasional effect became affectionately known as the 'signing-off' signal.

Robins conducted extensive control monitorings at such sites as open fields and concrete structures in several parts of southern Britain, well away from megalithic sites, but he never reported pulsing similar to that obtained at Rollright (and at certain other sites as described in the following main guide).

Readings intermittently resumed after the midsummer of 1979 and on into the autumn once more. The pattern of readings as recorded on our instrument was checked against sunspot activity for the period between October 1978 and December 1979 and a suggestive *negative* correlation was noted—peaks of apparent ultrasound intensity corresponded fairly closely with troughs in relative sunspot activity for the period.

It was interesting to have instrumental readings that seemed to indicate a genuine anomaly of some kind, and as word of these tentative findings got out, journalists and other media people began to join us at various sessions. At inactive times, when the ultrasound detector would remain stubbornly dormant, there was always the hint in visitors' attitudes that we had imagined or invented the pulsed readings, while those who witnessed some of the pulsing displays on the meter began to question whether or not the instrument was faulty, causing a spurious effect, an artefact. In a sense, it was a no-win situation. Nevertheless, while the apparent signal on the receiver was quite definite and certainly did occur, we were obliged to check for explanations other than ultrasound, the presence of which we could not in any case explain. The transducer of the receiver was designed to turn pressure waves in the air caused by ultrasound into electrical energy. As such transducers can also respond to radio signals, it was, naturally, screened against this, and in addition we took measures to satisfy ourselves that the effects we noted could not be due to radio signals. The only other possibility of false readings was that there was some fault within the instrument's circuitry. This meant that we needed to have the detector examined by independent engineers, and to test its reactions against a similar model. We attempted both these courses of action in 1980.

By the February of that year we were in a position to commence the logistically complex exercise of a month's almost continuous monitoring at Rollright. Shifts of stoic volunteers undertook a punishing monitoring schedule that included both day and night work in harsh winter conditions. We obtained permission to use the custodian's hut in the trees by the circle to provide the volunteers with sleeping accommodation. The opportunity was taken to introduce a wider range of monitoring of other possible energetic effects than ultrasound alone, and certain *psi* experiments were also conducted in the period. But we were most keen to see if 1980 produced a February peak in the apparent ultrasound activity as had happened in 1979. A second, slightly modified ultrasonic receiver was constructed in time for the exercise, which we called 'Operation Merlin 1' or OM1 (OM2 and OM3 took place later in 1980 and in 1981 respectively).

The day before OM1 was due to begin, Robins, myself, and other Dragon Project 'regulars' carried out a dawn ultrasonic monitoring session at the Rollright Stones as a marker for assessing subsequent readings by the volunteers who had not had any experience in the use of the instrument. At the King Stone our receiver displayed very strong pulsings of the needle, indeed similar to those of February 1979. We were accompanied by the BBC, who picked up nothing on their ultrasound tape-recorder. The project's instrument was taken to the BBC engineering training centre in Evesham, accompanied by Robins. There the circuitry of the device was given a preliminary visual examination. On his return Robins told the rest of us that the BBC engineers could find nothing that could readily explain the effects we were getting as an artefact caused by the machine. (However, in a letter written to one of the project's electronics people in March 1980, the head engineer at the Evesham centre expressed some doubts about the genuine ultrasonic nature of the readings he saw the machine indicate at Rollright. While he admitted that the instrument was sensitive to ultrasound, he was concerned that lower frequencies might in some way also be deflecting the meter.)

On 16 February the full-scale Operation Merlin session got under way at Rollright. While many other interesting research areas were successfully handled during this exercise, it proved something of a disaster from the ultrasound viewpoint. The new machine had serious design faults and soon malfunctioned in the harsh conditions. It had to be abandoned. Things did not go well for the original detector either. In his notes, the first monitor of the OM1 shift, Brian Larkman, commented, 'Unfortunately torrential rain and heavy wind on 22 February disrupted the [ultrasonic] readings severely and possibly damaged the detector'. Although through the following gruelling month readings were obtained from the instrument, they were erratic and there was no doubt in my mind that the ultrasound results obtained during OM1 could not be relied upon.

After OM1, we had the machine examined by an independent electronic engineering company. Among other potential problems, the examining engineer found the instrument to be rather dependent on voltage and the band-width of the tranducer to be too wide (1.5 kHz to 100 kHz), with significant peaking at 6 kHz, well within audible sound frequencies. He concluded that quantitative measurements on the machine had 'no value whatsoever' and that only general trends could be given any credence, and then with caution. At this stage, my initial optimism that an understanding of at least some energy parameters at sites could be arrived at fairly easily was dashed. If a machine like this, built by a person competent in electronics to a standard 'bat-detector' design could not be relied upon to give unequivocal ultrasound signals, how could we ever be sure of our findings? To this day, however, I am prepared to vouch for the fact that the results we observed up to February 1980 were definitely not due to audible sound components. We were fully conscious of the effects of speech, friction, and handling on the instrument and we carefully registered all background sounds against meter response. I am also quite sure that fresh batteries did not affect the overall pattern of meter responses, even if the instrument was overly sensitive to voltage supply, as this, too, was something we were wary of. (This factor seems to be present in some of the OM1 readings, however.) While we may have to discount intensity of the apparent signals obtained, their *occurrence* so selectively around dawn through 1978 and 1979, plus the important *inactive* periods, suggest the presence of some kind of authentic external stimulus, whether ultrasound or not.

A more carefully designed circuit was prepared by the independent engineers, and production of new machines was supposedly put in hand by one of our own electronics people. But during this period our original machines, together with project funds earmarked for the new instruments, were stolen. It was a sad and exasperating end to a chapter of the project's research, but it told me how difficult the task was that we had embarked upon. Nothing seemed as if it was going to come easy, and so it has proved.

Although disheartened and with little funding, the initial ultrasound anecdote the zoologist had supplied us with (Part One), coupled with the enigmatic earlier findings at Rollright, still seemed worth pursuing. Things did not immediately improve. We purchased two narrow-band receivers (40 kHz), but we never obtained any response on this frequency. Rodney Hale designed and constructed some new items of equipment, including two ultrasonic receivers, one of which could be switched to monitor radio signals in the same frequency band as any detected ultrasonic signals. The instruments covered the 25–40-kHz and 15–30-kHz ranges respectively and they gave audio output to headphones. He used them for the first time at Rollright on 22 June 1980, but there was no evidence of unusual signals. However, this was not surprising, as no equipment had picked up apparent ultrasound signals in June.

Later in the year, Hale did pick up a curious signal near the King Stone that seemed to be coming either from the ground or out of the sky overhead! But it was at 9.30 am on 4 April 1981 that Hale picked up what he is convinced was an anomalous ultrasound signal. It was

> a steady note of a single frequency. The signal strength was sharply directional when rotating the receiver in different directions, but did not vary rapidly when walking along with the receiver held at a constant angle. The signal was heard only in the area of the King Stone and over the brow of the hill.

He checked for radio signals but obtained 'no response at all'. Nevertheless, he went to a radio repeater station visible on the skyline from the King Stone area, but 'no unusual signals were heard on any of the receiving equipment. Observations ceased about 10 am (Hale, internal Dragon Project report).

As monitoring demands in other areas of investigation on the project increased dramatically, it became difficult to schedule time for further ultrasound sessions—the dawn requirement proved a particular problem in getting people on site. Consequently, only intermittent ultrasound work was carried out over the following years.

In 1986, the project was able to purchase a wide-band bat-detector type ultrasound receiver produced by Queen Mary College Instruments Ltd. This is tunable across the 10 kHz to 160 kHz range. I carried out extensive tests with it in a variety of non-megalithic environments. All that was ever picked up in these tests in the ultrasonic frequencies was the hiss of the machine on the audio output—unless an ultrasonic sound was deliberately generated. It was used at Rollright for the first time on the dawn of 10 January 1987. With two colleagues, I moved between the King Stone and the circle, trying a range of frequencies. At approximately 37 kHz I began to pick up a clicking signal at various points around the circle, at one point within it, and in a limited area on the road between the King Stone and the circle. While within the circle I turned 360 degrees to see if any particular source could be identified. I was startled to find that by far the strongest sound was produced on approach to the tallest stone in the circle (stone 1, Barnatt survey), on the northern side, nearest the roadside hedge. There was no doubt about this: the clicking sounds coming from the instrument reached a staccato crescendo as the instrument came up to the stone. This effect could not be reproduced at other selected stones in the circle. Further investigation revealed the remarkable fact that the effect on the machine was caused only by a metre-wide band about half-way up the tall stone. Moreover, this band ran right around the stone and the bat detector was affected by all sides of the megalith. Instrument response ceased when the stone's base and

PLATE 30 The tallest stone in the King's Men circle. On 10 January 1987, a band 1 m (3–4 ft) deep around the middle of this stone affected reception on a new Dragon Project ultrasound detector. Was it emitting ultrasound or some other strange effect?

top portions were monitored. An audio tape-recording was made before the effect diminished an hour or so after sunrise. The three of us felt that we had surely at last pinned down the elusive and inconsistent ultrasonic factor. But more frustrations were to develop.

Later in the morning further Dragon Project volunteers arrived, including veteran monitors, Roy Cooper and Rodney Hale. We told them what had happened and played the tape back to them. For a while switching on the bat detector merely produced the background hiss, but for a brief period just before midday, the effect returned. Once more, the key source proved to be the tall stone, and the frequency of clicks built up dramatically on increasing proximity to the stone as before. Everyone was mystified, but Hale dampened the excitement a little when he announced that he was as certain as he could be that the sound coming from the instrument was actually caused by positive feedback between the loudspeaker and the ultrasonic microphone. Another electronics expert who had joined the group concurred. I felt like giving up with ultrasonic receivers altogether—whenever they apparently worked, there always seemed to be some technical explanation other than ultrasound! But no one had any explanation for the obvious effect of the stimulus band around the stone. The effect could not be reproduced elsewhere.

When obtaining the rapid clicks at the tall stone, a hand placed across the collector horn would stop or drastically diminish the sound. I took the machine onto the road where a patch of reception occurred. On placing the instrument inside a car the sound on the machine ceased, and recommenced when it was brought out of the vehicle. This was repeated many times. All these results indicated that whatever was involved, there had to be *some* external component involved in the instrumental effect, feedback or not. Furthermore, when the 'signal' stopped shortly after noon it was impossible to create experimentally feedback on the machine, even by putting the volume at maximum.

Dawn monitoring at Rollright on two occasions in June 1987 produced no results on any frequency. Rob Stephenson, John Lobb, and David Aston of the London Earth Mysteries Group monitored the site in August and obtained short bursts of clicks from three stones (including the tall one) in the circle. The frequency range was 20–22 kHz, however, dangerously close to audible sound ranges. A dawn session in September produced no results, but a little activity was recorded in October.

Another dawn session was carried out on 10 January 1988, on the wild chance that some form of annual cycle was involved with the mystery stimulus. But nothing was received. I used the instrument for a dawn session at Castlerigg stone circle, Cumbria, in April 1988, but again there was no response on any frequency.

So the zoologist's anecdote remains an elusive factor. It seems clear to me, at least, that at Rollright if nowhere else, some kind of external stimulus can trigger off ultrasound receivers. It may be random as it appears to be, or there may be a long-term complex pattern our fragmentary monitoring schedule has so far failed to discern. But something odd is going on, even if at present it seems to be slipping through our fingers like quicksilver.

PATTERNS OF RADIATION

Radiation research has proved to be a more stable subject, if just as arduous. OM1 saw the opening of the concerted Dragon Project geiger-monitoring programme, though Roy Cooper had spent several months prior to that establishing background counts in the Rollright area and Oxfordshire generally. Our original geiger counters were extremely basic, requiring manual counting of audible bleeps. But the instruments were rugged, performing reliably (if slowly) as later cross-referencing with other, more sophisticated, equipment has shown. Work also went on across the country establishing background levels in all kinds of locations.

PLATE 31 Roy Cooper using a geiger counter at the Rollright Stones.

The radiation profiles of the King's Men and King Stone areas gradually took on detail. The King Stone habitually gave slightly lower readings than background, while the circle nearly always displayed average counts. In March and August 1981, though, technically trained and competent monitors observed surges of double the count rate for a period of a few minutes in each case. Different machines were in use in each incident. At that time we were unable to monitor site and environment simultaneously, so these two anomalies could have been due to sudden cosmic-ray showers—we had no way of testing if the surge of counts was occurring in the surrounding countryside at the same time as within the circle. But such a surge has also been measured at the Scottish circle of Easter Aquorthies (see Fig. 26), while its environment *was* being monitored, suggesting that isolated radiation bursts can indeed occur inside stone circles.

A less transient radiation anomaly became apparent within the area of the Rollright Stones: a section of the country road just where it passed by the circle gave consistently high readings—three or four times the average background count. It occurred for just a few hundred metres. We took samples of the road's surface material from both high- and normal-count areas, and Robins carried out dosimetric tests in

London. He reported similar (and normal) count-rates for each sample. So there was either something radioactive in the road's foundations, or else its course happened to run over a small deposit of radioactive material. At first we thought this latter option was the probable answer, as there are numerous cases around the world where ancient sacred places coincide with uranium deposits (see Part Three). But a highly detailed study in 1988 by Rodney Hale using new equipment has shown that the high-count area is so precisely defined by the edges of the road that the cause must lie in lower levels of the road's structure. It was purely because we were looking at the area in detail for the Dragon Project that this condition came to light.

Although nothing to do with the stones or the natural energies of the site, this chance findings has, ironically, proven to be one of the great gifts of insight the Rollright research has yielded. The clues came in 1980 and 1981 when independent reports were handed in privately to me by very reliable project members. Each person, unknown to the others, had undergone a paranormal experience on the very stretch of road that was particularly radioactive. Being the only person to receive this information, I was in a position to realize that we had a 'spook' road immediately alongside the circle. And it was radioactive. It took some time for the likely significance of this to sink in, but it coloured some of the later radiation work and initiated a chain of thinking that I will expand on in Part Three, where the accounts of the witnesses are given.

In 1988 Hale led a team from the London Earth Mysteries Group in two detailed radiation surveys of the King's Men site. Fig. 9 shows the combined result of the surveys. Why should there be patches of higher radiation in the area occupied by the circle? It is likely to be due to varying concentrations of radioactive matter in the soil and probably occurs everywhere, but radiation surveys of this detailed level are ongoing work on the Dragon Project and we will not be sure until similar studies are made of random pieces of ground. In the interim, though, it is interesting to muse over one of the findings of a leading British dowser (who has asked to remain anonymous) who was one of those selected to conduct surveys of the Rollright site for the Dragon Project. In 1980 he found 13 dowsing reactions within the circle that he described as 'small areas with points of force in them . . . I have no proof of what these are but for the moment I think they must be particles of meteorite that have struck the ground and buried themselves'. He had found similar points under 40 other churches, cathedrals, and stone circles. Could the higher radiation areas relate to such deposits? It is certainly the case that in many parts of the world people have, from antiquity, considered as sacred areas where meteoric fragments have struck.

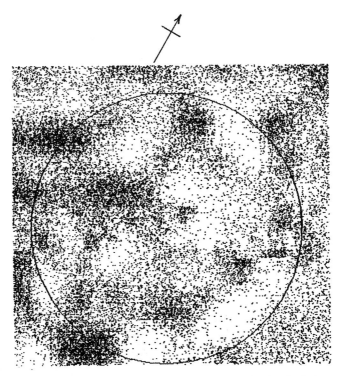

FIG. 9 Radiation survey of the Rollright circle expressed in dot density: the darker clusters of dots indicate areas of higher radiation counts. (The lower right-hand corner is filled with average values.) The circle on the diagram represents the ring of stones [*Rodney Hale*].

It will be seen in later pages that the study of radiation may have opened up what may be a most important understanding regarding the use of certain classes of prehistoric site.

PULSING STONES

Magnetism was another staple energy area the project wished to study at sites, especially in the light of the findings by Balanovski and Taylor at the Llangynidr Stone in Wales (site 15 in the main guide). But the cost of magnetometers to buy or hire was beyond the resources of the project in the early years. At that time, too, university departments were a little shy about loaning out equipment to an unorthodox group conducting work at remote places in tough, outdoor conditions. So this area of enquiry languished without attention by the project for a few years. As an interim experiment, however, biologist Harry Oldfield brought some brine shrimp to Rollright in the August of 1981. These creatures are very sensitive to changes in the geomagnetic field, and Oldfield decided to use them as biosensors within the circle to see if they would pick up any field variations around the stones. In the series of tests the shrimp did clearly cluster towards stones and led Oldfield to comment: 'Conclusions should not be drawn as yet, but the shrimps do seem to be aligning themselves over lines of force'.

Apart from this isolated experiment, no serious magnetic study was conducted until 1983. Then, in January, an article appeared in *New Scientist*. Charles Brooker, a retired BBC engineer and horticultural engineering consultant, had conducted a magnetic survey of the Rollright circle as part of a set of investigations he was pursuing privately. He used the stone circle only because it was the nearest suitable site for his purposes to where he hired his equipment. Brooker appeared to have made some discoveries during the course of his work that were relevant to the Dragon Project's interests. He claimed to have re-checked his findings with a second, more sensitive, instrument before publishing his brief *New Scientist* report. 'The average intensity of the

PLATE 32 Harry Oldfield placing a light-sealed container of magnetically sensitive shrimp at the King's Men circle, while two Dragon Project co-ordinators look on.

[geomagnetic] field within the circle was significantly lower than that measured outside, as if the stones acted as a shield,' Brooker noted (1983). On further surveying he found that the field broke down into bands of relatively higher or lower magnetic intensity within the circle. Closer examination revealed these bands not as concentric rings, but as forming a *spiral* of relative magnetic intensity. An extraordinary configuration for the local magnetic field to get itself into! But it did echo the findings of dowser Tom Graves, who, with a team of helpers, made a dowsing survey of the King's Men in the early 1970s (Graves, 1986). The dowsers claimed the presence of concentric bands of some dowsable force. In the light of Brooker's findings, I asked Graves if any members of his team had thought the dowsing pattern had formed a spiral rather than concentric bands. He replied that several had done so, but the majority consensus determined the published result. Brooker said the magnetic field variations he measured within the circle ranged from about 100 to 250 gamma.

The magnetic spiral, while fascinating, was somewhat bizarre. We got in contact with Brooker and learnt that he had also discovered something else that in many ways was more interesting—he had measured two stones in the west side of the circle, which were magnetically pulsing. They gave a cyclic variation of 50 to 60 gamma at a frequency of 40 seconds to one minute. This seemed the most suitable effect to check ourselves, and we resolved to get access to a magnetometer. Eventually, we obtained a flux-gate type machine with Hall probe on weekend loan from Birkbeck College, London, and, on 3 July 1983, a Dragon Project team assembled at the King's Men. Hale operated the equipment and apart from co-ordinator John Steele, a few regular project volunteers, and myself, there were a geologist and a physicist present to observe. The magnetometer was old and unwieldy, but it offered us our first opportunity to obtain direct magnetic measurements. The instrument used the oersted (Oe) as the unit of measurement. We were measuring in millioersteds (mOe). A horizontal line at 0 on the graphs in Fig. 10 would represent the earth's field, and we were seeing drops below that value, hence the mOe values are shown with a minus sign in front of them.

The weather was ideal—very warm and dry. We chose Stone 62 (Barnatt survey) in the north-west quadrant of the circle for the first 20-minute monitoring session (Fig. 10a). As the minutes went by, we could see from the magnetometer's meter that there was some fluctuation going on. But changes between 0 and -3 could be accounted for by variations of temperature within the circuitry of the instrument. Towards the end of the period, however, there were slightly larger shifts. We next went to an open field site about 3 km (2 miles) from the circle to conduct a control set of measurements (Fig. 10b). Here the graph

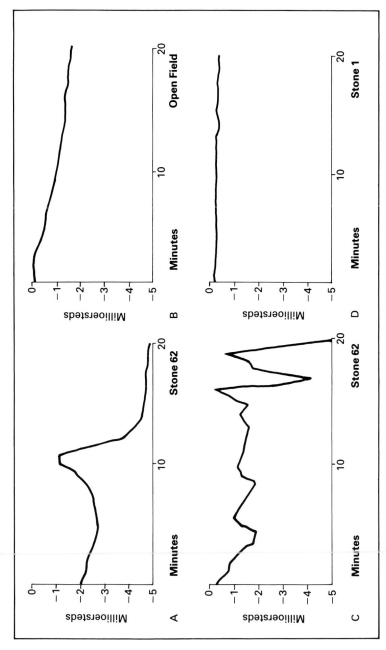

Fig. 10 Graphs showing magnetometer findings at two stones in the Rollright circle and one control site over 3 km (2 miles) distant. See text.

PLATE 33 Rodney Hale setting up the magnetometer for the first Dragon Project magnetic monitoring session in July 1983. The probe was inserted in existing natural holes in the megaliths, and had to be angled at approximately 70 degrees. Reliable readings could only be taken when everyone had vacated the area of the stone being studied.

shows a steady drift within the range of internal-circuitry variations. We returned to Stone 62 and hooked it up for another 20-minute session (Fig. 10c). After ten minutes we could see the choppy nature of the changes, but they were still within the bounds of instrumental 'noise'. But there was a big dip at 17 minutes followed by a peak. Then, almost at the end of the session, the readings began to drop and continued to do so until we had to change scale on the meter. At 23 minutes we had a reading of -28 mOe. No one present could account for the sudden, significant change. There had been no observable variations in the environment of Stone 62. Everyone was kept well away from the megalith; there were no cars or aircraft passing by. We then measured the tallest stone in the circle (Stone 1; Barnatt survey), which is nearest to the road. Fig. 10d shows a perfect reading without any anomalies. A stone on the southern side of the circle (Stone 37, Barnatt survey, where a 'shock' effect had been claimed four years earlier) also gave a smooth, normal graph. Before we left the site that day we measured Stone 62 again. It gave a level, anomaly-free reading.

Stone 62 was not one of those monitored by Brooker, so the two separate studies had shown three Rollright stones varying magnetically on the days the surveys took place. We did not know the cause, but we had a clear result.

By early 1987 the Dragon Project had two of its own magnetometers, and these have been used at many sites and their environments in Britain and Brittany, and a few of these findings will be mentioned later in this section. Hale and helpers conducted many trials with the new equipment at the King's Men during the course of 1987. By September the cautious Hale felt he could state that 'There seems to be some evidence growing of a fluctuating field within the circle relative to outside, changing over a period of hours'. But this work is not complete at the time of writing.

A magnetic survey of the circle for archaeological purposes was

FIG. 11 The areas of tone represent magnetic anomalies within the Rollright circle. See text [*Derived from survey by English Heritage*].

published by English Heritage in 1987: Fig. 11 refers to this survey and magnetic anomalies can be seen indicated in and around the King's Men. These could represent areas where there has been burning in the past, or some other disturbance to the ground causing a variation in the magnetism. The dowsed 'particles of meteorite' still come to mind, though.

In addition to this continuing high-sensitivity magnetic work, events at Carn Ingli (site 13 in the main guide, below) were to show me that other magnetic effects of stones could be discerned with relative simplicity merely by the use of a liquid-filled magnetic compass. This low-tech development has opened up new areas of enquiry into magnetic aspects of ancient places that will be discussed later in this book.

OTHER EXPERIMENTS

A large number of other experimental attempts at energy monitoring have been tried out at Rollright over the years—direct sensing in various modes by human beings; specialized audio-recording to pick up apparently paranormal 'electronic-voice phenomena' (EVP); Kirlian-style electrophotography and recording techniques; electric field measurements; resistivity work; infra-red photography; dynamic field study; electrostatic detection and the finding of radio anomalies, to mention some. Some biofeedback experiments were also undertaken, particularly with Audio Ltd's 'Mind Mirror' EEG monitor, which displays people's bi-cameral brain waves. The late Maxwell Cade, a leading expert in biofeedback, came on site at Rollright a number of times. He was able to make a preliminary observation that people tended to produce the deep theta and delta brain-rhythms when in the vicinity of certain stones at the circle. He had hoped to explore this further but, alas, he was denied the time.

But the list of experimental approaches could go on, and it would take the rest of this book to describe them all. This is not the place for a full account of the Dragon Project, and in any case some of these lines of enquiry produced no unusual results at all, and none indicated other than tentative anomalies. So I will make mention here of just two of these exploratory areas—infra-red and radio anomalies—to conclude this account of how the Rollright Stones have played host to the early efforts of a new branch of enquiry into prehistoric sites.

Infra-red photography has been employed at Rollright on a few, sporadic occasions. Infra-red (or heat) radiation is an electromagnetic radiation just beyond the red end of the visible-light spectrum. Special film can be obtained that is sensitive to the near infra-red, and can produce false-colour or black-and-white photographs of pictures taken in this wavelength. My first attempt at infra-red (IR) photography at

PLATE 34 Monitoring brain rhythms with a 'Mind Mirror' EEG instrument during dowsing work at the Rollright Stones. Left to right: the late Maxwell Cade, biofeedback expert and co-developer of the Mind Mirror; dowser Tom Graves; John Steele (partially obscured); Geoff Blundell; Isabel Cade (obscured), and psychic, Joyce Petchek [*Graham Challifour*].

PLATE 35 Unfiltered infra-red photograph taken of King Stone in April 1979. Note 'glow' effect around top and upper edges of the stone's silhouette. On the original this glow forms a column reaching up at angle from the stone to the top of the frame. The only frame on the reel of film with this effect, it catches the moment of dawn (sunrise off picture to left).

Rollright was on a clear April dawn in 1979. I took a set of exposures of the top of the King Stone at five minute intervals before, during, and for a while after sunrise. When the first roll of black-and-white IR film was (professionally) developed, I was astonished to see a curious 'glow' effect around the King Stone on the frame taken at sunrise. It appeared as a faint haze around the upper sides and top of the monolith, sloping off as a 'ray' to the left (north) until it disappeared off the frame. Was it some artefact of development? One of the project's occasional helpers was an IR physicist with Kodak UK, and he examined the film. Dosimetry tests showed that it was not a simple optical illusion. Other factors ruled out known refractive effects in the atmosphere that can occur at dawn. A suggestion that perhaps the rising sun's rays heated up the stone thus producing IR was dismissed on technical grounds relating to the wavelength sensitivity of the film's emulsion, which responded only to the 'near' or optical IR. The physicist could find no evidence that it was an 'adjacency effect' in which a dark edge can appear around light areas of a negative (seen as a corona of light around a dark area in a print) under poor development: the effect did not show on the pre- or post-sunrise sequences, nor anywhere else on the frame in question. Attempts to reproduce the apparent aura by taking IR photographs of King-Stone-shaped cutouts of black cloth against the sky failed. The effect was captured just once again exactly at sunrise a few weeks later at the King Stone, this time in misty conditions.

I carried out IR photography on subsequent occasions without anything unusual showing up, but a year or two later a professional photographer took a set of IR pictures around the Rollright complex during a dawn session of the project. A curious effect appeared on just one of his photographs: what looked like a small cloud could be seen apparently hovering about 4.5 m (15 ft) above the road between the King Stone and the circle. It was not observed visually by the photographer at the time. A similar effect was obtained by another photographer at the Kit's Coty dolmen in Kent (site 20 in the main guide, below).

IR equipment was brought in to see if the King Stone produced instrumentally detectable IR at dawn, but all results proved negative. The photograph remains unexplained, but caution must be observed in attempting to interpret it. I am undecided myself: I have done a great deal of both camera and darkroom work in photography, but have never seen an effect quite like that on the King Stone photograph. Close examination of the negative and print shows up detail that cannot be adequately reproduced. Nevertheless, there needs to be a lot more work done in this area before we can be sure a genuine phenomenon has been recorded.

A by-product of Hale's monitoring for ultrasound revealed a curious phenomenon with regard to radio propagation around the King's Men circle (but not inside), and around the King Stone. Normally when Hale held the aerial of his specially constructed broad-band radio receiver upright in the air, standard 'radio chatter' could be heard, and when he brought the antenna down towards the ground these signals faded away. But at certain times in highly localized areas, after the standard radio chatter faded, another signal could be picked up almost at ground level. While strongest on radio, these signals would sometimes produce or be accompanied by faint ultrasonic emissions as well. They seemed to run parallel to the ground for just a metre or so, appearing out of nowhere and going out of reception just as mysteriously. These highly localized 'blocks' of radio reception seem to defy the normal behaviour of radio propagation. They came and went, never reappearing in the same place and sometimes being absent for months. Hale managed to get an audio tape-recording of the signal, though, and he was convinced that it was artificial:

> I played my tape recording with an oscilloscope display. The modulation came in rectangular bursts at 50 Hz, precisely square-wave. The modulation shape during each burst was basically about 3 kHz, but of course with the ultrasonic demodulation process this is very difficult to interpret, but it looked very much like a man-made signal.
>
> (Hale, internal Dragon Project report)

The mystery was not so much the nature of the signal itself, as its behaviour near the circle. It could be some specialized, perhaps military, telecommunication we are ignorant of, but it currently remains unexplained. The only other place the effect has been detected is at a Bronze Age cairn site in the Wicklow Mountains in Ireland, described in following pages.

Rollright's spirit of place, its *genius loci*, has been a patient teacher, and those of us involved in this unorthodox work still make our way to the site from time to time, to learn a little more.

5 BRITISH SITES NORTH TO SOUTH—AN ENERGY GUIDE

In most instances this guide can be used in conjunction with only an ordinary road map, but certain sites will need the additional reference of an Ordnance Survey 1:50 000 scale map (recommended in any case). Even if the reader does not plan to use this guide to visit sites, the information contained in it is essential reading if the discussion in Part Three is to be followed adequately.

The site entries have been arranged in north to south order purely for simplicity's sake, and while the selection of sites probably does not include the totality of monuments where energetic phenomena have been measured or observed, it is undoubtedly the greatest single collection yet published, and many of the cases described are seeing print for the first time.

Every site entry includes a brief note on location, including reference to the appropriate Ordnance Survey (OS) 1:50 000 map sheet—the standard 'Landranger'-type map, and the monument's grid reference. (Those unfamiliar with the simple grid-reference system of location will find it explained in the margin notes of the OS sheets.) Each site description contains a general information outline on the place.

To date, the main emphasis of research into the possible presence of noteworthy energy effects at sites has been directed primarily at megalithic monuments—dolmens, stone circles, standing stones, underground stone chambers, dating respectively from third to first millennia BC—but the guide also contains a preliminary look at energy aspects of some holy wells and a few natural hill sites that were considered sacred places in ancient times. Although Christianized in the present era, the wells selected here were almost certainly considered important places for healing and religious practice from at least the first millennium BC, and probably earlier still.

1. TENGA, MULL

The Isle of Mull lies off Scotland's west coast, opposite Oban. The site is between the Aros to Dervaig road and the south-east end of Loch Frisa in the northern part of the island. OS 1:50 000 sheet 48. Grid reference: NM 504463.

Fig. 12 Map showing distribution of British sites described in the guide. (Other sites referred to in this book are not depicted.) The numbers relate to those given to each of the sites in the guide, and run in order north to south. Some towns are also indicated to help generally in site location.

Tenga is a stone circle in what archaeologist, Aubrey Burl, categorizes as a 'ruined but recognisable' condition. Four tall uprights and a fallen stone are all that are left to mark a ring that probably had a diameter of about 33 m (107 ft).

Fiona Way was one of the 'Gaia Programme' (see Part One) volunteers, who helped to compile a nationwide set of 'radiation snapshots' of British sites in the mid-1980s. The radiation picture obtained at Tenga was not anomalous, but a comment on Fiona's report sheet caught my eye: 'The stone on the E side deflects the compass needle'. I did not follow this up until a few years afterwards, when it became clear that we were finding other sites that had such magnetic stones. For the purposes of this book I asked Fiona to visit Tenga once more to compile a clearer picture of the magnetic effect.

The compass effect occurs around the two easternmost stones, one fallen and one still standing. Fig. 14 shows diagrammatically how the compass behaves around the two stones: north is at top of diagram. Fiona Way comments:

> The upright stone seems to have a reversed polarity through the north-south axis. It was my son who pointed this out to me; I didn't see it myself. Incidentally, when approaching this stone the needle started its movement about three feet away from it and was at its strongest at about nine inches and inwards.
>
> The fallen stone has a weaker reaction, a 20 degree deflection from north to east, the same movement as on the eastern face of the upright stone.
>
> There is a rocky outcrop about half a mile west of these stones, on the hillside, which seems the obvious place where these stones could have been quarried, so I took my compass over there. I checked all along the outcrop, and about halfway along came to a spot where the compass needle swung round into a complete reversal of polarity!

FIG. 13 The remaining stones (four standing, one fallen) of the Tenga circle. North is at top of diagram.

98

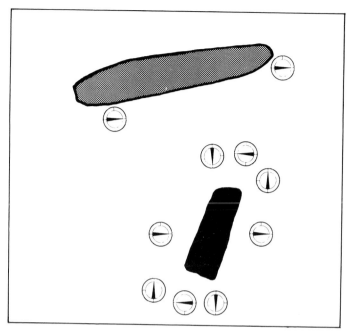

FIG. 14 The standing (black) and fallen (toned) stones in the north-east part of the Tenga site, with a diagrammatic depiction of the behaviour of a compass needle in their vicinity. North is at top of diagram [*After Fiona Way*].

The best-known site on Mull is the well-preserved Loch Buie circle (NM 618251), near the island's southern coast. The circle has nine stones, with a small outlying stone to the south-east and a nearly 2.7-m (9-ft) tall outlier 36 m (40 yd) to the south-west. This tall outlying stone has its long axis directed at the circle and according to Burl (1976) is 'well-placed...for observing the midwinter sunset'. Fiona Way has done a preliminary check of the site with a liquid-filled compass and found no reactions except on this tall outlier which 'gave a ten degree deflection to the east', an effect that seemed to occur along a crack on the western face of the stone. A ten-degree deflection is smaller than the effects referred to at other sites mentioned in this guide, however.

2. MACHRIE MOOR, ARRAN

The Isle of Arran is situated in the Firth of Clyde between the Scottish west coast and the Kintyre peninsula. The Machrie Moor complex of stone circles is on the west side of the island a few miles north of Blackwatersfoot. Access is by foot from the A841 coast road a little south of Machrie Water. OS 1:50 000 sheet 69. Grid reference: NR 910324.

A walk of a little over a mile from the A841 brings the visitor to a sweep of moorland, enclosed like an ampitheatre by mountains to the north, east, and south. The first clearly identifiable circle that is encountered is Machrie Moor 5 (MM5), a concentric double ring of squat granite stones. From this point the moor gently drops away and there is a dramatic panorama of the remains of circles composed of either small, grey-granite blocks or very tall sandstone slivers, like purple fingers pointing up out of the peat moss. There are at least eight visible circles scattered over the moor, one of which (MM11) had been completely submerged by the peat.

MM5 is clearly the 'special' circle of the group, being concentric and on the highest ground locally. Folklore also singles it out, saying the circle was built by the giant Fin MacCoul, and a stone on the outer ring is where he tied Bran, his dog, while he boiled a cauldron in the inner circle. MM5 also seems to be a little special in energetic terms. In May 1983 Dave and Lynn Patrick monitored several of the Machrie Moor circles, including MM5, with a geiger counter for the Gaia Programme. They also took background control readings and monitored a non-megalithic 'dummy site' for comparisons.

PLATE 36 Machrie Moor 5, also known as Fingal's Cauldron Seat, from the south-west.

Five of the circles (MM1, MM2, MM3, MM4, and MM11) gave average site readings 2 to 13 per cent higher than background, but MM5 gave a site average of 33 per cent above background. A non-megalithic 'dummy' site on Machrie Moor was 5 per cent above background. The Patricks had taken 20 readings within MM5—one hour of monitoring time—plotted onto the ground-plan. There was no mystery about why the site gave a higher average than anywhere else, and a third higher than background—the stones are radioactive granite, and there are 23 of them. But one stone, the tallest and the most westerly of the upright stones in the inner ring, is particularly energetic, giving readings 16 per cent above the next most radioactive stone in the double ring, and more than that for the other 58 stones monitored in the Patrick's study on Machrie Moor.

I took measurements at the site myself in April 1988, using new equipment, and confirmed that the MM5 stone did indeed give a moderately high natural radiation count (about 33 per cent above normal). Sceptics will shrug and say 'So what?' The fact is that this clearly special circle has within its circumference relatively high natural radiation zones. As a single example it would mean nothing, but as the radiation story unfolds over the following pages, it will be shown that this is not an isolated case, and I will argue that the megalith builders knew perfectly well the property of granite by their own sensitivities and empirical means, and found certain uses for localized environments of higher-than-background radiation.

But the Machrie Moor environment can display more dramatic energy effects, as was discovered by the chance observations of Paul Bennett, editor of the specialist journal, *Earth* (20 Stonegate Rd, Thorpe Edge, Bradford, W. Yorks.), and eight colleagues in February 1986. The group was camping near the Machrie Moor complex, with four of its members sheltering in a derelict house that had supposedly been built on the site of a group of standing stones. In the early hours of 3 February, the four individuals were awoken by glows and 'tubes' of light within the building and an accompanying 'deep humming noise'. The display lasted for approximately half an hour. Fifteen hours later, Bennett and a companion were seated in a van within the Machrie circles complex when

> a bright orange glow was seen on the summit of the mountain (Ard Bheinn), three miles away. A second or two later a ball of light rose up from the snow-clad hills and into the clouds, a hundred feet above. A few minutes later we saw the same ball of light again; on both occasions the ball of light was visible for two seconds at the most.
>
> (Bennett, 1986)

The eastern edge of Machrie Moor has a fault line running along it, at the foot of Ard Bheinn. We will see that stone circles are almost always located close to geological faults, areas particularly prone to the appearance of light phenomena.

3. LONG MEG AND HER DAUGHTERS, CUMBRIA

Situated north-east of Penrith. Take M6 junction 40 to join A686 to the east. Take Little Salkeld road and then Gamblesby road. A surfaced track off this (at NY 570365) leads to the circle and farm. OS 1:50000 sheet 91. Grid reference: NY 571373.

Long Meg is a 3.7-m (12-ft) tall sandstone pillar, 18 m (60 ft) south-west of a huge circle of granite stones, the Daughters, 109 m (358 ft) across its longest diameter. Long Meg has three faint prehistoric images carved on the side facing the circle—a cup-and-ring mark, a spiral pattern, and a set of concentric semi-circles. There are said to be 68 stones in the circle, with 27 remaining upright. The heaviest, on the south-south-west of the circle, is estimated to weigh 28 tonnes. A pair of double stones at the south-west indicate a probable entrance. Recent air photography has revealed the existence of a huge earthen enclosure, hitherto invisible, to the north of the circle, which meets with and fits exactly the flattened northern segment of the stone ring (Soffe and Clare, 1988).

Photographer and Earth Mysteries researcher John Glover, has noted that at midwinter sunset the tip of Long Meg's shadow reaches precisely to the far side of the circle, the length of the shadow enhanced by the slope of the ground on which the site is situated. This suggests that the height of Long Meg was very precisely decided upon by the builders of the site. Glover notes (1980) that it is as if Long Meg is attached to her Daughters by an umbilical cord on the winter solstice.

Legend explains the stones variously as a witch coven turned to stone, or Long Meg and her secret lovers likewise petrified. The stones are said to be uncountable, and anyone trying to damage them will suffer retribution. It is recalled in folklore that when one Colonel Lacy attempted to remove the megaliths by blasting, a terrible storm erupted and the workmen fled. There is also a tradition that if a piece was ever broken off Long Meg, she would bleed.

The stones were monitored for radiation by Jim Taylor Page for the Gaia Programme in August 1983. The average of the readings of the site as a whole were 16 per cent above the background readings, but this was not the real story. Jim Taylor Page found that the stones in the north-west quadrant of the circle were giving considerably higher readings than stones elsewhere in the ring. He wrote on his report that

PLATE 37 Part of the north-west quadrant of the Daughters circle. The stone in the centre of picture is one of those that has small areas on its surface emitting almost constant streams of radiation.

this increase of readings 'was very dramatic and made them stand out as exceptional without doubt...Certain spots on their surfaces were emitting almost continuous radiation'. These stones were, naturally, granite, but they were yielding up to double the count rate of some other granite stones in the ring, and substantially higher than any of those in other quadrants.

I conducted further geiger readings in April and August 1988, with the same instrument used by Taylor Page as well as new equipment. I soon determined that there was nothing unusual in radiation terms about the location itself, but was able to confirm the high readings off *parts* of some of the westernmost stones, two of which are indicated in Fig. 15. With an instrument that gives 15–25 cpm in normal radiation conditions, I was getting at least one count a second from certain points on one stone.

I frankly do not believe that stones with this characteristic were placed in the circle without their handlers knowing about it. How and why we will discuss later on, but a hint is in the experience had by Mr Peter Thornborrow, a Historic Buildings officer in a county archaeological service, who gave an account of it at a chance meeting with researchers, Andy Roberts and David Clarke, in July 1988 (not on site). In the 1960s Thornborrow had visited the site while on honeymoon. It being a cool, overcast September day, his wife of two days did not want to leave the car to explore the circle, so Thornborrow went for a walk inside the ring of stones alone. He began to feel 'dizzy' and

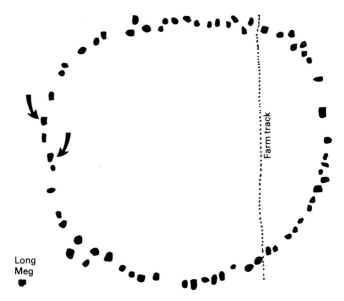

Fig. 15 Groundplan of the Long Meg and her Daughters site, Cumbria. North is at top of diagram. Two stones containing points of noteworthy radiation are arrowed. See text.

'really strange'. It was as if he was 'not really there' or, he felt, really more as if the stones '*were not in the same time*' he was in (my emphasis). He moved over to a stone—he could not recall which one—and leant on it. 'I got an electric shock off it,' Peter Thornborrow stated. It was an experience he would never forget, and his legs were shaking as he returned to his wife, to whom he said nothing about his adventure.

Apart from the ubiquitous shock-from-a-stone (Thornborrow claimed that he did not realize it was quite a common experience), a key comment in this man's account was the reference to a sense of a time shift. There is no way he could know what is being published for the first time is this book—that zones of high natural radiation can induce in some people a sense of *time slip*, as we shall discover.

4. CASTLERIGG, CUMBRIA
The circle is located about a mile east of Keswick in the Lake District of north-west England. Take easterly course out of town centre; recommended approach road to site (signposted) from town outskirts on way to A66. OS 1:50 000 sheet 89. Grid reference: NY 292236.

The siting of this magnificent stone circle is amongst the most impressive in Britain: a stunning skyline of rugged Lakeland hills surrounds the location. The site is well preserved, with its stones forming a flattened circle 33.5 m (110 ft) across its longest diameter. Inside the main ring of stones is a mysterious rectangular setting of ten stones, often referred to as 'The Cove'. A gap flanked by two large stones in the north of the circle was probably an original entrance. In all, there are 38 surviving stones at the site, the heaviest weighing around 15 tonnes.

The late Alexander Thom showed (1967) that there were potentially seven sun or moon alignments involved at this site, some of them related to the ground-plan geometry. At midsummer the sun sets over Latrigg, north-west of the circle, at which time, as John Glover (1980) discovered, the tallest stone at the site throws a dramatic and regular 'shadow path' far into the valley. This line of shadow from the circle would probably extend for 3 km (2 miles) were it not for the intervention of a modern conifer plantation. Folklore tells that the stones of Castlerigg are a council of Elders, petrified in the midst of their deliberations.

In 1978 I carried out ultrasound monitoring over three dawns around the midwinter solstice as part of a Dragon Project visit to Castlerigg. For two dawns no signal was registered, but on the third there was distinct pulsing of the meter needle when in the vicinity of one of the stones that marks the midwinter sunrise within the circle (Devereux, 1979). As this result was with the project's first ultrasound detector, it has to be viewed with the qualifications indicated earlier. Nevertheless, it was most impressive to witness at the time and difficult to explain purely as an instrumental artefact. It certainly seemed as if some external stimulus was present, and located around a particular stone. Another dawn ultrasound monitoring session, using the new equipment referred to earlier, was carried out on 13 April 1988. The frequency range between 20 kHz and 120 kHz was scanned with no results.

Castlerigg and its environment were monitored by Lesley Park in 1983 as part of the Gaia Programme, and another geiger counter study was made on 13 April 1988. Nothing anomalous in radiation terms was noted in either investigation.

During the 1988 visit, all the Castlerigg stones were checked for anomalies with liquid-filled compasses. Only one of the 38 stones affected the compass needle. This was the westernmost stone, now leaning outwards from the circle. Its inwards-facing side strongly deflects a compass needle in one area, and attracts it in another. Due to its leaning position, the outer side of the stone cannot be properly checked. No magnetometer study has yet been carried out.

PLATE 38   Midwinter sunrise over Castlerigg circle. The smaller stone on the sunrise alignment, on the far side of circle to the camera, was the one around which apparent ultrasound was picked up over the 1978 winter solstice.

The stone circle was the focus for an outstanding energy display in the early years of this century. Writing in *English Mechanic and World of Science* in 1919 a Mr T. Sington described an experience he and an acquaintance had around Easter some years earlier. They were returning to their hotel in Keswick in darkness and on foot after an ascent of Helvellyn:

> When we were at a point near which the track branches off to the Druidical circle, we all at once saw a rapidly moving light as bright as the acetylene lamp of a bicycle, and we instinctively stepped to the road boundary wall to make way for it, but nothing came...It was a white light, and having crossed the road it disappeared...
>
> We then saw a number of lights possibly a third of a mile or more away, directly in the direction of the Druidical circle, but, of course, much fainter, no doubt due to distance, moving backwards and forwards horizontally; we stood watching them for a long time...Whilst we were watching, a remarkable incident happened—one of the lights, and only one, came straight to the spot where we were standing; at first very faint, as it approached the light increased in intensity...But when it came

PLATE 39 *Above*: The westernmost
stone in the circle (leaning, on the far
right in this view) is the only one at the
site to affect compasses.

PLATE 40 Castlerigg's 'magnetic stone'
strongly attracts and deflects a
compass needle at different points.

close to the wall it slowed down, stopped, quivered, and slowly went out, as if the matter producing the light had suddenly become exhausted. It was globular, white with a nucleus possibly six feet or so in diameter, and just high enough above ground to pass over our heads...

The lights we saw all moved horizontally, never vertically, or at an angle; they moved in opposite directions at the same time, therefore they were not affected by any air currents.

Sington concluded his account by wondering why the site of the stone circle had been selected. 'Suppose, owing to some local condition at present unknown,' he mused, 'such lights have occurred from time to time near the site, they would have attracted the attention of the inhabitants, who, awestruck, would have attached great significance to them, and might then have selected the site as a place of worship or sacrifice' (*ibid.*). This was a remarkably perceptive idea for its time, and it is only now, well over 60 years later, that research—and that 'alternative'—has begun to address the issue.

Sington wondered if other sites were so affected: the indications being put forward in this present book have, unfortunately, come too late for him.

5. TWELVE APOSTLES, ILKLEY MOOR, WEST YORKSHIRE

Ilkley Moor (part of Rombalds Moor) rises above Ilkley, on the A65 north-west of Leeds. The edge of the moor can be reached by car from Ilkley, but access to the site, out on the eastern side of the moor, is by foot. OS 1:50 000 sheet 104. Grid reference: SE 126451.

Ilkley Moor has a concentration of prehistoric stone features. Most famous are the many Bronze Age rock carvings to be found on natural boulders scattered across the moorland. No one has an inkling as to the meaning of these mysterious patterns of the past.

There are also at least eight stone circles within this moorland fastness, a interesting fact considering this is a region with few stone circles generally. But if we are to suspect that the unusual light phenomena we are now becoming aware of, the natural but remarkable earth lights, were held to be important to the spirituality, the cosmologies, of the megalith builders, then the concentration of sites on Ilkley Moor can be readily explained. This and adjoining moorlands are a focus for strange lights (Devereux, 1989). Dozens of cases have been logged by local and regional researchers between 1975 and 1986 alone. Clusters of lights, lightballs, flashing lights, and columns of light have all been reported by many people over the years.

A typical example is a case involving the natural outcrop known as

PLATE 41   The Badger Stone, Ilkley Moor—one of the many rocks on the moor with Bronze Age glyphs carved into it. There are around 100 theories for these markings. To add one more—could they be related to the strange light phenomena that seem always to have haunted this moorland? [*Jerry Hardman-Jones and Brian Larkman*].

the Cow and Calf Rocks on the edge of the moor overlooking Ilkley itself. At 7.50 pm on 26 September 1982, three women on the outskirts of Ilkley saw a bright 'glare' above the rock outcrop. It was caused by two balls of light falling out of the sky, dropping behind the rocks, which are on an active fault zone. At one point in their descent, the light balls became stationary. They made no noise and lit up the surrounding landscape. The Cow and Calf Rocks have been the scene of a number of other light phenomena, especially luminous columnar effects.

Few people are ever in the depths of the moor in darkness, so there is scant record of anyone observing how light phenomena might interact with the stone circles. But by a fortunate chance one incident was witnessed at the Twelve Apostles circle. This is a ring of 13 stones, but several are missing. They describe a true circle within a low circular bank 15.9 m (52 ft) across. In 1976 a team of the Royal Observer Corps were out on the moor engaged in exercises. Three members of the team claimed to have distinctly seen a bright white object travel over the moor and come to a stop and hover directly above the Twelve Apostles circle.

A geiger survey of the circle by Brian Larkman and John Barber in October 1983, and a preliminary magnetic check with compasses in

PLATE 42   The Twelve Apostles circle, Ilkley Moor, Yorkshire [*Simon Roberts*].

1988, revealed no anomalies. There have, however, been reports from a number of people claiming to have received shocks off some of the stones.

6.   BAILDON MOOR, WEST YORKSHIRE

Baildon is north of Shipley, near Bradford. The flat moor commences north of Dobrudden Farm. OS 1:50 000 sheet 104. General grid reference: SE 140400.

This moor is really part of the southern reaches of Rombalds Moor, only 7.5 km (4–5 miles) south of Ilkley Moor. Like its northern neighbour, Baildon Moor is home to a range of megalithic features—at least 16 boulders with prehistoric carvings and a selection of cairns dot its wastes. Two stone circles have also been discovered on its south-west flanks; one at Brackenhall Green (SE 130390) and another at SE 132401. Like the whole Rombalds Moor area, the Baildon district has had some startling outbreaks of light phenomena over the years. One sighting, on 24 July 1984, implicated both stone circles, as local investigator, Paul Bennett, discovered:

110

Mrs A.R. and one of her sons noticed a bright, red elongated object moving across their field of vision above Baildon Moor. Going outside their house to get a better look, they noticed that the object seemed to be more a cluster of four, maybe five, smaller spheres moving in conjunction with one another. Looking westwards from the witnesses' position, the objects seemed to be moving northwards on the far side of Baildon Hill where Shipley Glen and Brackenhall Green lie. As it edged its way slowly on, the formation of lights gradually curved in direction following the shape of the hill, until they attained an easterly direction. Eventually, the formation flew out of sight behind the other side of the hill. The maximum distance the witnesses were from it was 0.7 km and its height above ground was estimated at 150 feet.

(Bennett, 1985)

Bennett carefully studied local geology maps and he was able to relate the course of the formation to local faulting and the position of the stone circles, as shown in Fig. 16. Bennett also notes that in 1980 several

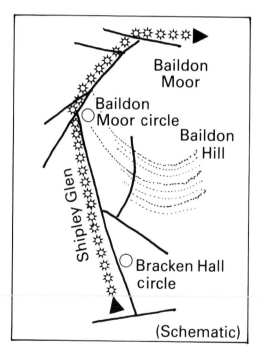

FIG. 16 Stone circles and faults (bold lines) on the edge of Baildon Moor shown diagrammatically in relation to the course of a light phenomenon (depicted in star symbols) described in the text [*After Paul Bennett*].

sightings of light phenomena were reported in the immediate vicinity of the Brackenhall Green circle, and 'some appear to have gone right above it' (*ibid.*)

The phenomenon we are beginning to discern could be expressed in rhyme, though admittedly not poetry:

> First was the geology,
> then came the lights;
> next appeared people,
> and then the sites.

Time, perhaps, to move on to the next site...

7. BIG MOOR, DERBYSHIRE

The moor is located about 13 km (8 miles) south-west of Sheffield. Best access for the Barbrook circles is off the A621 where it crosses Ramsley Moor. Stile and footpath onto Big Moor on west side of road at SK 281752. OS 1:50 000 sheet 119. General grid reference: SK 270750.

Seven stone circles (including one on Ramsley Moor adjoining to the east, just across the A621) are concentrated on this moor: Barbrooks I–V, Brown Edge, and Froggatt Edge sites. In addition, there are several individual standing stones. Archaeologist John Barnatt, has shown that five of the circles form spatial relationships with one another so that regular geometric figures are formed such as isosceles and right-angle triangles. Furthermore, this geographical geometry relates 'to the landscape in a strange way as if they underlie the formation of this area of the moor' (Barnatt, 1978).

One of the best preserved circles is Barbrook I, fortunately the site most easily reached from the A621. It is visible a short distance to the right of the trackway leading from the main road, and has twelve stones forming a ring 14.5 m (47.5 ft) across its widest diameter. A low, eroded earthen bank encircles the stones. Most of the stones are under 60 cm (2 ft), but one is 1 m (3.5 ft) tall. Five of the circle's stones yield solar alignments on key days in the year, and a sixth is formed between the circle and a cairn on a nearby ridge. This site also has a number of distant outlying stones that create further astronomical alignments with the circle.

Barbrook II is only a very short walk from Barbrook I, but the other sites lie further into the moor. Preliminary geiger counter and compass checks at Barbrook I revealed no obvious anomalies. The whole Big Moor area, so geometrically configured by the megalith builders, is another focus for light phenomena, along with its surrounding districts,

PLATE 43   The low stones of Barbrook I, Big Moor.

just like the moors of the Ilkley and Skipton areas. The location of these high incidence areas of unexplained light phenomena in the Pennines have emerged from the research of Project Pennine, directed by David Clarke and Andrew Roberts, and is described more fully elsewhere (Devereux, 1989).

One incident occurred on 9 September 1987, when two witnesses independently reported observing a red light over the uninhabited Big Moor. A search was conducted by mountain rescue teams over the whole area and no explanation was found.

Froggatt Edge, where one of the stone circles is situated, is said to be haunted by a 'white lady' ghost. I have shown that these tend to be associated with areas of light phenomena incidence, and have suggested they are a faintly luminous gaseous discharge from the ground (*ibid.*). All actual eyewitness accounts match this interpretation.

8.   MOEL TY UCHAF, CLWYD

On the north-west slopes of Cadair Bronwen, above Llandrillo, which is on the B4401 south-west of Corwen, North Wales. Minor road leading towards mountain branches east off B4401 at a telephone box a mile north of Llandrillo. Road passes through a few gates then becomes steep, rough track. Negotiable by vehicle to gate and wall at SJ 049379, thence progress by foot along track. Circle on knoll to left (north-east) of track. OS 1:50 000 sheet 125. Grid reference: SJ 056372.

Only when the brow of the knoll is almost breached do the 41 low, boulder-like stones of the site come into visibility. It is this subtle placing within the landscape that has probably helped to keep the 12-m (40-ft) ring of stones in its well-preserved state. The stones are contiguous, giving a rather different appearance from a stone circle with spaced megaliths, and the site is usually described as a 'ring cairn' (a retaining kerb of stones around a burial mound). It is doubtful, however, if the site was ever covered by a mound, though there may have been a burial cist in the centre of the ring, now marked by a depression in the ground. Professor Thom found the ring to have an interesting ground-plan geometry, a view endorsed by the geometer Keith Critchlow, who considers (1979) the site to be 'perhaps the most geometrically sophisticated of all the Neolithic structures'. Its location is superb: it overlooks the valley of the Dee—which also marks the major Bala Fault here—and a sunset viewed from the site is an unforgettable experience, with a succession of blue mountain ridges

PLATE 44   Radiation monitoring at the Moel ty Uchaf circle.

fading into the golden western horizon. 'The resonances from the cathedral-sized plateau on which this small circle sits echo all around the huge encompassing bowl of hills,' Critchlow (*ibid.*) observes.

This stone ring and the mountain on which it is positioned (in the Berwyn range) were at the centre of a truly remarkable display of geophysical energy in 1974. At 8.30 pm on 23 January people in a wide radius of the mountain heard a curious explosion that was followed minutes later by a tremor, which was felt up to 96 km (60 miles) away and recorded by the Global Seismology Unit of the British Geological Survey in Edinburgh. Curious lightball phenomena were seen local to Llandrillo and over a wider area both before and after the event. Villagers in Llandrillo reported seeing red disks of light encircling the mountain prior to the subterranean explosion; just before the actual event an astronomer in East Anglia, hundreds of miles to the east, saw a blue fireball tracking west, its course being monitored by another observer in Coventry; amateur astronomers reported what they thought to be a meteor travelling south, and fireballs were reported over the Irish Sea and the Bristol Channel. In other words, aerial lights were seen at all compass points around the North Wales area. Police saw mysterious lights in the area immediately after the rumbling explosion, and coastguards at Holyhead on Anglesey saw a flaming tadpole-shaped object about an hour afterwards (Buckle, 1974; *Guardian*, 1974; *Tanat Chronicle*, 1980; Devereux, 1982).

The event made headline news, the prevailing hypothesis being that a great meteorite had struck Cadair Bronwen—especially as there had been reports of 'fires' and descending 'streaks of light' over the mountain at the time of the explosion and tremor. The next day police made a 'token' search of the mountainside and found nothing. The RAF made flights over the area and found nothing. Scientists were dispatched to scour the mountain, and also found nothing. The evening following the event, while searches for its cause were just getting under way, various witnesses reported seeing a multicoloured disk of light hovering over the Berwyn range. Dr Roy Lilwall, of the Edinburgh Seismic Unit, was quite sure the substantial tremor had not been caused by a meteorite; if it had been, he pointed out, it would 'have had to weigh several hundred tons' (*The Times*, 1974). The huge scar such an object would have made on the mountain could not have been missed by anyone. There was no scar. There was no meteorite.

As the truly anomalous nature of the event became apparent, news of it fell from the headlines. The last 'scientific' explanation I heard of the event was that an earth tremor had taken place coincidentally at a time a meteoric fireball was seen. While technically almost true (there were in fact multiple-light phenomena over a period bracketing the time of the explosion), this, of course, sidesteps the true nature of the geophysics involved. Had its actual occurrence not been so widely established, I suspect the event would have been dismissed as never having happened at all. Therein lies the weakness of our science and, indeed, of some branches of modern ufology. Never mind if no other light-phenomena event ever happened, this incident, centred around the locality of Moel ty Uchaf, certainly did take place, and remains unexplained to this day. That lack of explanation is a measure of our ignorance.

A few days after the geophysical display, while Keith Critchlow was at Llandrillo, preparing to study the Moel ty Uchaf site, he fell in with scientists who were investigating the mountain. Critchlow happened to notice that a geiger counter switched on in the vicinity of Moel ty Uchaf gave extraordinary readings. It was this observation, passed on to me by personal comment from Critchlow, that caused the Dragon Project to include radiation monitoring at sites as part of its activities.

Moel ty Uchaf and its environment were monitored for radiation in 1979, 1981, 1982, and 1983 (as part of the Gaia Programme) with a variety of equipment. In March 1982 a gamma counter showed that the ground around the bases of the northern stones (rather than the stones themselves) consistently gave readings averaging 53 per cent higher than background (or even the centre of the ring itself), and different equipment on other occasions has tended to show the north-north-west segment of the ring, and the ground immediately to the north, to give higher-than-average readings. In the 1983 study, though, this variation was not apparent. But at no time have truly exceptional results been forthcoming. If the 1974 readings were not the result of instrument malfunction, we have to look for some link between the geophysical activity and a startling increase of radiation in the vicinity of the site. At a guess, the general higher radiation on the northern perimeter of the ring might indicate an escape point for radon gas, which was aggravated at the time of the tremor. If this is the case, it would be my further suggestion that the placing of the ring on such a radon-emission point was no accident.

9.   DYFFRYN ARDUDWY CHAMBERED CAIRN, GWYNEDD

The cairn's remains are just off the A496 to the east, in the village of Dyffryn Ardudwy, situated between Harlech (to the north) and Barmouth on the north-west coast of Wales. Signposted. OS 1:50 000 sheet 124. Grid reference: SH 588228.

What now confronts the visitor to this site are two dolmen structures in the midst of a flat area of stone cobbles. Originally, this Neolithic long cairn was a single dolmen chamber inside a wedge-shaped cairn,

PLATE 45   One of the exposed chambers of the Dyffryn chambered cairn.

to which a second dolmen in its own round cairn was added shortly afterwards. Pottery fragments from near the first dolmen suggest a date of around 3000 BC for the site.

The chambered cairn sits directly on the Mochras Fault, by far the most important one of the entire area. In 1904 and early 1905 there was an outbreak of well-documented light phenomena along the fault (McClure and McClure, 1980; Devereux, 1982, 1989). My own analysis of the outbreak has shown the incidence of reported lights to have increased dramatically with proximity to faulting (Fig. 17). The outbreak occurred in a period of increased seismicity in Wales, some epicentres during which were close to this general area, which has a history both of seismicity and unusual light phenomena stretching back centuries.

Dyffryn was one of the 'hot spots' for the lights along the Mochras Fault. This is an eye-witness account of a Dyffryn event that occurred in January 1905:

> The first form in which it appeared to me was that of a pillar of clear fire quite perpendicular. It was about two feet wide, and about three yards in height. Suddenly another small fire began by its side some two yards distant...and increased rapidly until it assumed the same size and form...And as I gazed upon them I saw two arms of fire extending

117

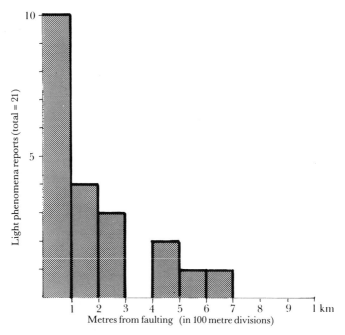

Fig. 17 Histogram showing the dramatic increase of reported light events with proximity to faulting during the 1904–5 wave.

upwards from the top of each of the pillars...I saw smoke ascending from the pillars, and immediately they began to disappear...the fire became small and went out. It was a very wonderful fire.

This phenomenon can have been only a few hundred metres at most from the chambered cairn and, of course, the fault. Similar luminous columns were reported by other local inhabitants in the area. Balls and rods of light were also seen, mystery glows on the mountains, and all the other forms associated with earth light phenomena.

The remains of other important megalithic monuments dot the area, haunting the local fault lines.

10. MITCHELL'S FOLD, SHROPSHIRE

The site is situated approximately 19 km (12 miles) south-west of Shrewsbury, just north of a country road connecting Chirbury and the A488. A track to the site leads from the country road at a sharp bend a mile to the east of the hamlet of Priestweston. Vehicular access is barred by gate at end of track leaving an easy walk to the site. OS 1:50 000 sheet 137. Grid reference: SO 304983.

This circle measures 27 m (88 ft) across and has about 16 surviving stones, of which 10 are standing. The monument is in an impressive position, commanding sweeping views to the north-west and over-looked by Corndon Hill to the south.

The primary legend associated with the site is that it was a place where a magical white cow could be found that gave milk 'to all the honest and good folks of the neighbourhood'. But one day a witch called Medgel or Mitchell brought a sieve and tried to milk the cow dry. The cow saw what was happening and vanished, while the witch 'was turned into one of those stones' now forming Mitchell's Fold ('fold' in local dialect means farmyard). There are numerous variants of this theme. No one seems to know which stone is the petrified witch: Grinsell (1981) suggests it was a now missing central stone, which best accords with some versions of the legend (and the nearby Marshpool circle does have a central stone), while Janet and Colin Bord (1976) think it may be what is now the tallest stone on the site.

PLATE 46 Mitchell's Fold circle. The tall stone can affect a compass needle.

119

Whether the witch stone or not, the 1.85 m (6 ft) pillar on the eastern side of the circle does possess a 'magical' quality—points along one of its outer edges will strongly affect a compass needle. The other stones in the ring do not seem to affect the compass significantly.

Radiation readings have been taken at the circle and its surroundings in 1983 and 1987. No startling results have been forthcoming, but it does seem the circle occupies one of the lower-level radiation spots in the immediate environment (measured to half-a-mile radius in the cardinal directions). In the April 1983 work, the site averages registered lower than the collective environmental averages in terms of both actual readings and computer-'weighted' readings (Devereux and Mullard, 1983). (It is possibly of significance that all sites so far found to have 'magnetic stones' tend to be rather low in radiation counts compared with their surroundings.)

While radiation monitoring the circle in August 1987, Geoff Bird and his colleagues from the Bristol-based QUEST Earth Mysteries group were interrupted by a group of people who had been present at the

PLATE 47   The outer edge of the tall stone strongly affecting a compass.

PLATE 48   *Right*: The remains of the Fairy Stone, Shropshire.

circle a few days previously—on the night of 17 August. These people claimed to have witnessed a ball of light at an estimated distance of 50 m (55 yd) from the circle, and later to have witnessed lightballs emerging from the ground around the stones. Although Bird felt these people to be intelligent and sincere, 17 August was the night of the 'Harmonic Convergence', a New Age international event, so expectations for 'something' to happen would have been high; moreover, we do not have the names of the people concerned, so the anecdote has to be treated with extreme caution. It is worth recording, however, because it is a fact that on that evening UFO research groups received reports of UFOs from a wide area of Britain—though this may have been due to meteor showers. The date was also preceded by what the British Geological Survey call a 'sonic event' in Gwynedd, Wales, on 15 August, and followed by seismic activity near Liverpool on 20 August.

11.   THE FAIRY STONE, SHROPSHIRE

Situated on Clunbury Hill, by the B4385 close to the village of Clunbury, in the centre of a triangle formed by Knighton, Ludlow, and Lydham. OS 1:50 000 sheet 137. Grid reference: SJ 372798.

A stump of rock only 75 cm (2.5 ft) tall is all that remains of this former standing stone, which was also known as The Devil's Stone. The girth of this stump, though, suggests that the former monolith must have been substantial in size—probably used as a local landmark, as a parish boundary crosses the hill by the stone. The stone is granite with quartz veins, and almost certainly got to these parts as a glacial erratic.

The existence of the stone was uncovered from the archives by researcher Jonathan Mullard, while conducting an intensive study of the sites and traditions of Shropshire. The stone had a long tradition of fairy lights associated with it; they were said to appear at certain times of the year. The legend would seem to relate to actual folk knowledge of the site, because Mullard was informed by an elderly woman living locally that she recalled her grandfather telling of an encounter with the lights. Returning home one evening across Clunbury Hill, he saw the whole area around the stone filled with small lights of a gaseous appearance bobbing up and down a short distance above the ground. Not wanting to go out of his way, the man walked through them. He found that any lights he happened to touch against adhered to his trousers. He briskly brushed them off, but found when he got home that the fabric was scorched. The woman had actually kept the trousers up until a decade or so before talking with Mullard!

As so often the case, these lights were equated with fairies. Mullard consulted a geological map of the area and found that the stone stands on a fault.

12. BURTON DASSETT HOLY WELL AND CHURCH, WAR-WICKSHIRE

Burton Dassett is about 18 km (11 miles) south-east of Warwick off the northerly side of the A41 near Fenny Compton. The well is on the left-hand side of the lane approaching the church. OS 1:50 000 sheet 151. Grid reference: SP 389515.

Formerly a market town, Burton Dassett was decimated centuries ago by the ravages of the Black Death and tenant evictions. All that remains today is a scattering of cottages and farms and the fine church with its holy well. The present All Saints church is twelfth century, but it occupies a much earlier site. It now forms one of the attractions of the Burton Dassett Hills Country Park.

Little is known about the stone-enclosed holy well other than that its waters were used for baptisms, but Janet and Colin Bord (1985) suggest that it was

> probably also...credited with healing properties and much used when Burton was a thriving community. The area's history stretches back to Saxon times...We can speculate also that the holy well has been in existence at least since Saxon times.

The location was at the centre of an extraordinary outbreak of light phenomena in 1923 and, briefly, in 1924. Brilliant lights danced round the region, with activity definitely focused on Burton Dassett. David

PLATE 49 Burton Dassett church.

PLATE 50 Burton Dassett holy well.

Clarke and Granville Oldroyd, working from contemporary sources, describe (1985) one event that took place in February 1923:

'I frankly did not believe a word of it,' said Mr White... 'but out of sheer curiosity we paid a visit to the hills a few nights ago. It was about seven o'clock, and when we had been there a short time Mr Shearsby said "Here it is!" We turned round, and about 200 yards away was a strong and dazzling light... It was a perfectly lovely sight, and it held us fascinated.'

'We could feel it hover around,' said Mr White '... I had my field-glasses and was able to get a close-up view. It was a kind of reddy-blue mixed, but beautifully blended... Later, when we saw it round Burton Dassett church, there was a tinge of orange colour. There was nothing whatever to be afraid of, and I have decided to go again, hoping to see it. I was a sceptic before, but I swear I have never seen anything like it.'

Many people saw the lights, including journalists specially despatched to view the phenomena. Some detailed and careful accounts were filed.

The hills around Burton Dassett are riddled with minor faults, and the church and well are positioned immediately adjacent to the Burton Dassett Fault itself. There is scattered evidence that light phenomena have been associated with other wells and churches. Lights were reportedly seen at a well near Hay-on-Wye on the Welsh border with Herefordshire, and 'white lady ghosts' are associated with a number of wells in England and Wales. The churches at Linley, Shropshire, near Lough Erne, Northern Ireland, and Gardenstown, Grampian, Scotland, are amongst several where lights have been reported. But it is research still requiring further work. It would also be interesting to know how many ancient churches stand on faults.

13. CARN INGLI, DYFED

Carn Ingli is one of the westernmost peaks of Mynedd Preseli, overlooking Newport on the north Dyfed coast. The route allowing shortest (but steep) foot access is via a minor road that runs south-east from Newport towards Cilgwyn. There is a fork in the road where it begins to climb into open country. The right-hand branch (marked 'No through road') becomes unfenced immediately beneath the east flank of Carn Ingli. OS 1:50 000 sheet 145. Grid reference: SN 063373.

The Preseli hills were like a magnet to prehistoric people, and scattered on and around them are remarkable monuments dating from the Neolithic period through to the Iron Age. It was argued by a geologist in the 1920s that the bluestones of Stonehenge originated here, and has been repeated like a catechism in archaeological literature ever since. The hills have a remarkable atmosphere about them, and dotted along their ridge are jagged peaks or 'carns'—eroded clusters of igneous rocks—that stand out starkly. Carn Ingli is one of the most spectacular of these rugged peaks, around which people long ago built stone walls that today mingle with its crags almost as natural extensions. These tumbled walls loop down the steep slopes of the carn, enclosing series of terraces. Archaeologists would date them to the Iron Age, but in truth no one knows when human beings first draped Carn Ingli with necklaces of stone.

'Carn Ingli' can be translated as 'The Peak of Angels'. It got this name because of a sixth-century Irish holy man, St Brynach, who was a friend and contemporary of St David. Brynach founded a number of churches, most important among them the one at Nevern, a hamlet tucked away in remote country just north of Mynedd Preseli. The

PLATE 51   The rugged central peak of Carn Ingli. People can be seen clustering round one of the areas of reversed magnetic field there.

church enclosure seems cut off from the modern world, with an almost palpable sense of the sacred about it. The churchyard has a 'bleeding yew', which always has a sticky, blood-red wound in its trunk, and a remarkable Saxon cross. Even more ancient stones, one carved with the archaic Celtic script called ogham, have been incorporated into the surviving Norman structure of the church itself. A clear view of Carn Ingli can be had from immediately outside the churchyard, and it was on this peak that St Brynach lived the life of a hermit and communicated with spiritual beings—with angels.

Carn Ingli has taken on significance from a 'site-energy' point of view because of an incident that was reported early in 1987 to 'Llowarch', the pen-name of Keith Stevenson, a columnist for the *Cambrian News*. A young man and his girlfriend were driving near Carn Ingli when the woman complained of curious sensations, as if she was being subjected to waves of some kind of force that seemed to be originating from the peak itself. The couple parked the car and approached Carn Ingli on foot, but the closer they got, the more strongly the girl felt the sensations. Becoming concerned, they retreated to the car and left the area. The young chap told his father, a local man, about the experience, and that is how Stevenson first got to hear of the affair. In May 1987, he was able to visit the place for himself, and during investigation

125

of the craggy height he and his colleague, Richard O'Gorman, noted strong compass anomalies at points amongst the rocks. Stevenson contacted me about the matter, and later in the summer of 1987 I visited Carn Ingli.

I was certainly able to confirm the magnetic anomalies. The compass needle moved tens of degrees off magnetic north in some places, while in a few it turned full south—180 degrees deflection. This could be obtained just by holding the compass in mid-air at certain points. The startling effect, as explained earlier, is caused by minerals contained in the rock being 'frozen' into the direction of the earth's field at the time the rocks were formed. At Carn Ingli it is possible, in effect, to sit in an actual archaic geomagnetic field—as it was when the poles were reversed.

Over several visits, with my wife and numerous colleagues, compass checks were conducted at many of the other Preseli carns. Nothing remotely comparable to the effects at Carn Ingli were discovered. In fact, only a very mild effect was found in one place on one carn. Carn Ingli really does seem to be special on Preseli, as far as present investigation has indicated. Was this field effect the secret of the place,

PLATE 52 Compasses held in mid-air point full south at various places on Carn Ingli.

causing it to be picked out as special by prehistoric people, and by a Dark Ages holy man who knew he could have visions and enter altered states of consciousness there?

I mentioned the phenomenon some time afterwards to an inspector of English Heritage—the body in charge of ancient monuments in England—when we both happened to be in the Preseli area. He was duly impressed when he accompanied me to the site and saw the compass response. He later informed me that he had visited Carn Ingli again, in the company of two women. One of these suddenly complained of hearing sounds that seemed inexplicable under normal circumstances. All three of them, he told me, saw a rainbow effect in the sky over the peak. 'That was at least symbolic,' I suggested. 'It was more than that,' the inspector replied. 'At the time we saw it, darkness had fallen!'

14. GORS FAWR, DYFED

The circle stands just to the south of Mynedd Preseli near Mynacloch-ddu, alongside a country road between Maenclochog on the B4313 to the west and Crymych on the A478 to the east. OS 1:50 000 sheet 145. Grid reference: SN 135294.

PLATE 53 Gors Fawr circle. Note how height of stones decreases towards the far side of ring from camera.

Gors Fawr is on a broad tract of land in sight of Carn Meini on the Preseli range. Sixteen fairly low stones survive to describe a circle about 22 m (72 ft) in diameter. The stones get gradually taller in order towards the southern part of the circle—a grading phenomenon noted at some other stone circles. Compass checking of this ring revealed no magnetic anomalies at all.

Two larger stones, each about 2 m (6 ft) tall, stand roughly 130 m (140 yd) to the north-east, presumably outliers to the circle. They stand 13.7 m (45 ft) apart, and Professor Thom calculated that the alignment they form marks the midsummer sunrise over Mynedd Preseli. The stone nearest the circle yielded no magnetic anomalies detectable by compass, but the further, north-east, stone of the pair strongly deflects a compass needle along its south-west side.

It may be fortuitous, but this 'magnetic stone' is so shaped that a kind of seat is formed on its southern side—a factor considered further in Part Three.

15.   THE LLANGYNIDR STONE, POWYS

On the north bank of the Usk, between Abergavenny and Brecon. The B4560, signposted to Llangynidr, branches off the A40 at a sharp bend just south of Bwlch. Left off this, then first right. The stone is on the private Glanusk Estate, and permission is required. OS 1:50 000 sheet 161. Grid reference: SO 156204.

If Carn Ingli alerted us to look for magnetic anomalies by the simple

PLATE 54 *Left*: The two outliers of the Gors Fawr circle, forming a midsummer-sunrise alignment. The furthest stone from camera is magnetic.

PLATE 55 One side of this outlier has a notable effect on a compass needle. Note the seat-like shape of stone.

means of the compass, it was the Llangynidr monolith (or Llwyn-y-Fedwen Stone) that brought the possibility of megalithic magnetic anomalies to the fore in the first place and, indeed, was the first old stone to attract orthodox if adventurous scientific attention from the point of view of 'energies'.

The stone is the tallest in the Brecon Beacons National Park area at 4.3 m (14 ft), and it weighs 20 tonnes. It stands with an idyllic backdrop of the Usk Valley and the mountains beyond. It came to notice in the mid-1970s when the author Francis Hitching was writing a book and making a TV documentary (both with the title *Earth Magic*). He had the Welsh master-dowser Bill Lewis, who lives at Abergavenny, to dowse a stone for him. They chose the Llangynidr stone as it was relatively close by. Lewis dowsed the spiral of energy as he often does on standing stones. He urged Hitching to see if a scientist could be persuaded to take measurements at the stone. So Hitching contacted Professor John Taylor of King's College, London. Taylor felt that Lewis might be responding to small changes of magnetism in the stone, and supplied Hitching with a gaussmeter for reading magnetic field strength, and a young Argentinian physicist called Eduardo

PLATE 56 The lichen-encrusted Llangynidr Stone.

Balanovski, then at Imperial College in London. Hitching picks up the story (1976):

> What Balanovski found surprised him very much.
>
> After checking the background levels and setting the meter at zero, he pointed the measuring probe at the stone. The needle on the dial shot up, showing an anomaly far greater than the few thousandths or hundredths of a gauss that would have been normal...
>
> Balanovski has no doubt that the basic anomaly...is significant: 'The point is that a water-diviner told us about it, and we went there and found something measurable. It may be the stone contains, geologically, the reason for the anomaly. Or it may be caused by something we don't yet understand. But I do not personally believe that the stone was accidentally chosen or accidentally placed. The people who put it there knew about its power, even if they didn't know about electro-magnetism.'

This initial sortie was sufficiently interesting to entice Taylor himself to the stone a short while later, and he and Balanovski conducted further work with Lewis at the monolith. Lewis was filmed marking with chalk the places on the stone where he dowsed 'energy nodes'. When the gaussmeter probe was passed down the stone, it did register increases of magnetism at the marked points—there seemed to be 'a very strong field on and around the stone, which seemed to fall in bands' as Hitching (*ibid.*) put it. It was a very impressive demonstration. Taylor urged caution, pointing out that much more work would need to be done to be sure of such reactions, but that if confirmed by further work, the findings would be 'very remarkable indeed'.

Some time after the publication of Hitching's book, I checked with Taylor to see if there had been any more work done at the standing stone. He said further readings had been taken, but they had 'proved a little contradictory' (*The Ley Hunter*, 1977). Nevertheless, the experiment as described by Hitching did serve to augment interest in energy research at prehistoric sites, and put magnetic monitoring on the Dragon Project's agenda. Ironically—for various reasons, such as the late appearance of magnetometers on the project and the fact that the monolith is not readily accessible—there has been only one brief, preliminary Dragon Project visit to the Llangynidr stone. No radiation anomalies were noted, and a period of magnetometer monitoring did not show up any immediately anomalous results. But this work *was* perfunctory, and serious further work is still required at this site.

16. MAEN LLIA, POWYS

Located in the heart of the Brecon Beacons, 16 km (10 miles) south-west of Brecon. Visible on the east side of country road between Heol Senni and Ystradfellte, 9.6 km (6 miles) due south of Sennybridge (on the A40). Easy foot access to stone. OS 1:50 000 sheet 160. Grid reference: SN 924193.

This impressive megalith stands alone in the unspoilt grandeur of the Brecon Beacons hill country, between the narrow country road and the upper reaches of the River Llia. It is 3.7 m (12 ft) tall, almost 2.7 m (8 ft) wide, yet less than 8 cm (4 in) thick—a large, flat slab. Its axis is virtually true north–south, and points down the valley, from the far end of which Maen Llia appears as a distinctive marker precisely on the visible horizon.

According to folklore, the stone visits the River Neath (Nedd) 'when it hears the cock crow'. It is curious that the legend selects the Neath, which is on the other side of a mountain to the west, when the emerging streams of the River Llia are so close to the monolith. On 4 April 1987, two Dragon Project magnetometers were used to monitor the stone and the local environment simultaneously over the sunset period. (An

earlier attempt to get to this remote spot at dawn—'when the cock crows'—resulted in arrival just at the point of sunrise, thus not allowing a comparison with the pre-sunrise period.) Monitoring took place for half an hour before sunset to half an hour after. In Fig. 18 we can see that the magnetic readings for the stone and the environment 'parted company'. Perhaps the stone 'goes for a walk' at sunset too!

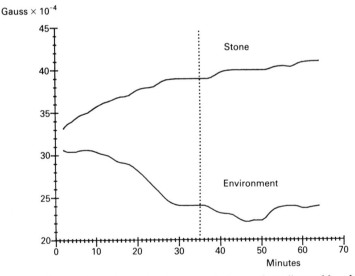

Fig. 18 Smoothed graph showing the 'parting of ways' of magnetic readings at Maen Llia and in its environment over a sunset period. The sun actually set at the 35-minute point of the monitoring period, marked by vertical broken line [*Rodney Hale*].

PLATE 57 *Left*: The slab-like Maen Llia, with its axis running north–south.

PLATE 58 The gnarled Long Stone in Gloucestershire.

17. THE LONG STONE, GLOUCESTERSHIRE

The stone is just inside a field next to the country road between Minchinhampton (south-south-east of Stroud) and Avening at Hampton Fields. OS 1:50 000 sheet 162. Grid reference: ST 884999.

This stone stands just over 2.5 m (8 ft) tall, and has two large and several smaller holes in it, all thought to have been caused by weathering. A smaller stone that stood near it has long since been placed in a nearby wall to form a stile. Archaeologists think that both may once have formed part of a chambered mound.

A number of folklore themes have attached themselves to this stone. The principal one is that it runs around the field when it hears the Minchinhampton clock strike midnight. But it was also considered a healing stone in times past, and mothers would pass babies suffering from whooping cough or rickets through one of the larger holes. Folk memory has it that years ago someone tried to move the stone by attaching several oxen to it, but 'something held it firm'. The stone is, furthermore, associated with the appearance of a 'black dog' in local tradition. These curious, supernatural creatures are said to haunt specific spots around the British Isles, and an understanding of the motif is yet to be arrived at. Actual observation down the years is one obvious option.

In June 1988, during a course on practical dowsing held by the British Society of Dowsers in Stroud, Alan Lovejoy visited the Long Stone with many of the other delegates, who included several engineers and a physicist. As he approached the Long Stone, Lovejoy switched on his Mersmann geomagnetometer. He reported in the regional Earth Mysteries journal, *Gloucestershire Earth Mysteries* (1988):

> As I got to the Long Stone the ground in the immediate vicinity was indicating between 5 and 7 on a scale of 10. Readings from the Long Stone itself took the needle completely across the scale, past 10 in a band approximately one foot deep, some 18 inches from the ground...The instrument indicated zero on the rest of the stone.

Lovejoy tested a stone in a nearby wall, where he got a reading of zero. Lovejoy was at pains to mention in his report that he had not recalibrated his instrument since doing indoor work earlier that day, but the *differences* being recorded were legitimate, even if the actual values were not.

After ten minutes, the 'band' on the Long Stone was again monitored, and this time the reading there was zero. A number of the dowsers present laid their hands on the stone for several minutes. Measuring the monolith along the inside edge of one of the holes, Lovejoy saw the needle beginning to creep up from 0. Within five minutes or so of the dowsers' 'charging' of the stone, the geomagnetometer readings had risen to 7 on the meter.

Although this may indicate an interesting human–stone interaction (see Part One), it is also reminiscent of the varying low-level magnetic readings at Stone 62 at Rollright (above) and may instead have been part of the odd magnetic phases megaliths seem to display.

The megalith does not seem to affect a compass held near it.

18.   AVEBURY, WILTSHIRE

Fourteen and a half km (9 miles) south of Swindon and the M4. Junctions 17 (via Chippenham), 16, and 15 (via Marlborough) south off the M4 all lead to Avebury. The A361 Devizes road actually cuts through the great monument. Museum, bookshops, restaurants, and an inn. OS 1:50 000 sheet 173. Grid reference: SU 103700.

This vast site, 427 m (467 yd) in diameter, is one of the greatest prehistoric sites in Europe. It consists of a massive ditch-and-bank circular enclosure (the actual henge), containing the remains of a stone circle around its inner lip, which in turn contains the remnants of two smaller circles. The southernmost of these inner circles had a very tall centre stone known as the obelisk, now destroyed; the northern inner circle has now almost disappeared, and the remains of its central feature is known as 'The Cove'. The stones, some weighing 40 tonnes or more, were brought from the surrounding Downs. Avenues of stone were connected to the south and west entrances of the henge (and possibly to the north and east also) but only the southern one, Kennet Avenue, has any lines of stone left standing or restored. Religious bigotry led to the destruction of many of Avebury's stones in earlier centuries.

The small village of Avebury lies on the western edge of the henge, actually sprawling into the enclosure, and a main road passes through the henge. So mighty is this site, however, that it somehow manages to accommodate these intrusions. A relatively unspoilt Neolithic landscape surrounds the henge, with Windmill Hill to the north-west, the staggering artificial mound of Silbury Hill to the south-south-west, and important Neolithic stones and long barrows all around.

Legends and lore have attached themselves to Avebury henge itself and to some of the other sites in the overall complex. But an interesting feature is that several accounts seem to refer to actual experiences or events. Janet and Colin Bord, for instance, report (1976) that

> In Avebury...some of the cottage walls incorporate stones from the circle and there have been reports of 'strange happenings' in those particular cottages. Exactly what has happened is not specified, but occurrences of a poltergeist nature are likely.

The stones of 'The Cove', for example, were once used as end walls of a cottage built between them. During World War 1, the author Edith Olivier was driving through the henge at dusk when she heard the sounds and lights of a fair amongst the stones. Telling someone about this later, she was informed that it had been half a century since a fair had last been held there. The Bords (*ibid.*) also report another incident in which eerie small figures were seen flitting amongst the stones in moonlight.

But a more specific, contemporary report of a light phenomenon has recently (1987) come from a lifelong inhabitant of Avebury, whom I will not name as she is a very well-known member of that community. She is a solid, reliable countrywoman in her middle years. While walking her dog one October evening in 1983, around 10 o'clock, she saw what she momentarily took to be the moon over the south-west quadrant of the henge. She was on the road just inside the west entrance to the henge. The 'moon' was, in fact, a soft, yellow-white orb of light that silently drifted over the bank and ditch of the henge,

PLATE 59 The south-west segment of Avebury henge. A light was seen to pass over these stones and to descend to the grass within the arc they form.

PLATE 60 A set of five crop circles in a field immediately north of Silbury Hill at Avebury. Mysterious circles of flattened and swirled corn have been reported from various places in southern Britain over recent years. They seem to cluster in certain locations, Avebury being one of them. This set of circles appeared in the summer of 1989 in the area where 'orange lights' were seen to 'disappear into the ground' during the same period.

descended past the stones in the outer circle of the south-west quadrant, and settled like thistledown onto the grass just inside the arc of megaliths. 'It just went out,' the witness said. 'It made no sound at all' (referred initially to me by Andrew Collins; personal communication from witness).

Requests for permission to carry out energy monitoring at Avebury have met with a stalled response at the time of writing. But a preliminary compass-anomaly check of just a few of the stones in the complex have so far proved negative. Don Robins (1985) reported picking up apparent ultrasound in the henge ditch in May 1979. In recent years Avebury has been a focus for the curious 'crop circles' appearing mysteriously in fields of cereal crops. In 1989 orange lights were reportedly seen entering the ground in the self-same locations.

19. BATH (AQUAE SULIS), AVON

The Roman baths and ruined temples, which overlay the prehistoric sacred springs, are enclosed within a museum-display precinct in the centre of Bath, close to the abbey. Museum, bookshops, entrance fee. OS 1:50 000 sheet 172. Grid reference: ST 751648.

Bath has Britain's only hot springs. They were in use at least 7,000 years ago, and in the Iron Age they were dedicated to the Celtic goddess, Sulis.

The Romans were strongly drawn to what was clearly a major Celtic shrine. They identified Sulis with one of their own goddesses, Minerva, but maintained the presence of the Celtic deity rather than supplanting her. They built a temple, bathing, and theatre complex at the springs. One of the many statues of the religious centre is known to have been dedicated to Sulis by a *haruspex* or diviner of the old Etruscan tradition called Lucius Marcius Memor (Scullard, 1979). A pediment above the entrance to the Sulis–Minerva temple depicted a so-called 'Gorgon's head'. Though this impressive, Celtic-style stone effigy (Fig. 19) does have writhing hair, it also has a moustache—an unusual attribute for a goddess! Jacquetta Hawkes (1973) felt that it more likely represented the Celtic sun-god, with flames rather than snakes as a hairpiece, and added 'in looking at what is certainly the finest example of the monumental sculpture of the romanized Britons, we are seeing a creation which expresses something of the spirit, of the imaginative vision of the ancestral Celts, of...prehistoric Britain'. Roman walling enclosed Aquae Sulis, but as archaeologist Barry Cunliffe (1985) has noted, the area 'is very much smaller than Roman country towns...and suggests that the wall, rather than being a city wall may

PLATE 61 The Great Bath in the Roman complex.

FIG. 19 The so-called 'Gorgon's head' found at Aquae Sulis. See text. [*Author's drawing*].

have been a *temenos* boundary defining the religious area'. Although on the fringes of the Roman empire, Aquae Sulis was a sacred site of significance.

Rock musician Maggie Stewart, a native of Bath, is involved with the history, nature, and present usage of the sacred waters, and writes a vigorous account of them (personal communication, 1988):

> Our ancestors came here generation after generation to gain spiritual enlightenment, knowledge, healing and to pass through the entrance to the Otherworld. For Bath is built over hot springs which have been the focal point for worship, divination, prophecy, necromancy and healing for many thousand of years. These springs...are situated in a truly magnificant setting nestling in a bend of the River Avon with cliffs rising on either side, amidst hills which up until quite recently would have been heavily wooded. The valley floor would have been marshy, with alder and willow groves from which the hot steamy vapours of the springs would have issued. A truly magical site conjuring up amazing images for our ancestors. Here they could commune with the Earth Goddess, the presiding deity being known as Sulis which in Old Welsh means an opening, gap, eye or orifice; all names associated with the topographical features of these springs. They were and still are acknowledged to be an entrance to the Otherworld, that world the Celts travelled to via the underworld [to which] these springs were known to be an entrance...and also a gateway where the spirits of the ancestors and other realms could float back through the channel of the priests and priestesses to commune with the living.

> Despite various problems to do with amoebae being found in the spring water in 1978 and the spa bathing facilities being closed down, people are still gathering here to experience whatever is needed for their

personal development. Much research has been done in the last few years and this now corroborates the mythological reality with archaeological and geological findings.

Detailed geological surveys have now discovered that the waters originated with ancient rain falling on the Mendip Hills which seeped deep into the carboniferous limestone to be warmed by the natural heat emerging from the Earth's core to something between 64–96° C. From here the water flows along a major thrust fault forming an aquifer which allows some of the water to spread laterally beneath the impervious shales, marls and clays of the Lower Lias series which forms the floor of the valley at Bath. Under tremendous pressure the waters rise to the surface where the strata are faulted and one of these known as the Penny Quick Fault passes through Bath. It is through fissures in this that the thermal waters ascend to become the hot springs of Bath, emerging in three places: the King's Spring (46.5° C); the Hetling Spring of the Old Royal Bath (49° C), and at the Cross Bath Spring (40° C).

The springs are rich in some 43 different minerals including iron, magnesium, copper and potassium and are also radioactive. Interestingly, they are completely non-sulphurous.

From these recent findings we can assume that these hot springs have been a feature of the landscape for many millenia so that by the time the Romans arrived in the first century AD they would have encountered a religious cult centre of some long-standing and importance.

PLATE 62 Hot, sacred spring water overflowing from the reservoir at Bath through a Roman arch.

PLATE 63 *Right*: Kit's Coty House, Kent.

Regarding the radioactivity, in 1903 R.W. Strutt found 'appreciable amounts' of radium in iron deposits left by the hot springs; the presence of radium in the water was confirmed by Nobel laureate, Sir William Ramsey (Williams and Stoddart, 1978). I have monitored the main spring water with a geiger counter and found it to have high natural radioactivity (relative to background levels), very much in keeping with levels found at a variety of sacred sites elsewhere, as Fig. 28 in Part Three clearly shows.

20. KIT'S COTY HOUSE, KENT

Approximately 5 km (3 miles) north of Maidstone, just to the west of the A229. The dolmen lies on a footpath a short distance north of the Aylesford–Burham minor road off the A229. OS 1:50000 sheets 178 or 188. Grid reference: TQ 745608.

The visual effect of this dolmen is marred by the metal railings hemming it in on all sides. The tallest of the three upright stones is 2.4 m (8 ft) high; the capstone is still in position and measures 4 m (13 ft) by almost 2.7 m (9 ft). Aerial photographs have revealed what appear to be the remains of a mound 55 m (180 ft) long that once surrounded or covered the dolmen.

PLATE 64 A filtered infra-red photograph of Kit's Coty. Note curious, cloud-like haze hanging over the dolmen and mixing with the nearby hedge [*Bernard Gowing*].

Numerous folktales surround Kit's Coty House ('coty' actually means 'house'), among them the beliefs that the structure was assembled by four witches, and that a personal belonging placed on the capstone at the time of the full moon will disappear if the owner circumambulates the monument three times.

Hearing of the exploratory infra-red photographic work on the Dragon Project, Bernard Gowing decided to try for himself. He took a series of filtered, infra-red pictures of Kit's Coty. Only one of them showed an anomaly, reproduced here. The photograph shows a curious, cloud-like effect lying just above the dolmen and mingling with the tops of the nearby hedgerow. The effect was not visible to the naked eye, Gowing states.

This apparent effect bears marked similarities with a curiously localized cloud appearing in an infra-red photograph to be hovering over the road between the King's Men and the King Stone at Rollright (see the Rollright Stones section, above).

21. STONEHENGE, WILTSHIRE

The henge is in the fork made by the A303 and the A344 5 km (3 miles) west of Amesbury, itself 11 km (7 miles) north of Salisbury. Bookstall, amenities, entrance fee. OS 1:50000 sheet 184. Grid reference: SU 122422.

This famous site has had many phases of construction and alteration, from the early third millennium BC to as late as the second century BC. The first features were the henge itself—the circular bank and external ditch 110 m (360 ft) in diameter—containing a ring of curious holes, and the Heel Stone, a huge block of sandstone that is now beside the A344. Later in its evolution, the Welsh bluestones were brought on site and went through various arrangements; an earthen avenue was built to (or from) the spot, and the huge upright and lintels formed by the relatively local sarsen stones were put up. The handling of the stones was incredibly sophisticated: each of the lintels on the outer ring was gently curved to make a complete circle, and there were mortice-and-tenon joints to hold them onto the uprights. Some of the bluestones had tongue and grooving!

Now fenced off most of the time to the general public, viewing is only at certain angles and from a certain distance (said to be because of erosion caused by the great numbers of visitors), and permission has to be sought to gain access to the stones to carry out particular investigations. A body of lore has attached itself to Stonehenge—the stones were brought from Ireland by Merlin; they are giants dancing; they have healing properties; and they cannot be counted.

One of our urgent concerns in 1987 was to check magnetically the bluestones. If they had come from Preseli, where we had noted the

PLATE 65   Stonehenge. The smaller upright stones are the bluestones.

143

marked compass anomalies at Carn Ingli (above), could they be magnetic? Was that the reason they were brought such a distance? If this was a story-book instead of an account of research, the answer would have to be positive. But reality is always more difficult than that. We did not get a single flicker of our compass needles! The bluestones seem to be stoically non-magnetic. We did not conduct any magneto-meter studies. In the course of our deliberations, however, Paul McCartney became concerned that the bluestones he was seeing at Stonehenge did not match those he had noted during his exploration of Preseli. In mentioning this to a number of archaeologists later, I received such comments as: 'I wouldn't be at all surprised if they are not from Preseli', and 'Really? I am glad to meet someone else who shares my opinion!', and so on. Perhaps it is time to test this article of faith. Even though a bluestone was found in a river near Haverfordwest near Preseli in 1988, it does not mean that the stones originated on Mynedd Preseli—they might have been from elsewhere in Wales, or over from Ireland as the legends claim, for Haverfordwest could have been on any route eastwards.

Radiation monitoring carried out in July 1988 showed there to be no unusual emissions of radioactivity at Stonehenge. Quite the opposite, in fact, with some of the stones giving less than background counts. So far, there have been no energy anomalies found at Stonehenge that can be detected by instruments. But there have been a few noteworthy observations.

Amongst the more interesting of these was an event witnessed by A. Moncrieff Davidson in the late 1940s. He was positioned on a track tangential to the north-west side of the henge awaiting a partial eclipse during sunrise on 20 June, the day before the solstice, a phenomenon he wanted to film. The weather was 'normal for the date and hour' as he and his wife waited for sunrise. Suddenly there was a report like a clap of thunder and 'a ball of fire' hit the ground ten yards (9 m) ahead of them. It disappeared and left no mark (personal communication). Such a lightball event is very rare in its own right, but for it to happen at Stonehenge, virtually at the solstice, and at the time of a partial eclipse, beggars the imagination!

If that is an example of light at Stonehenge, here is one of sound. In 1983 Gabriele Wilson, a niece of the late Robert Graves, placed herself inside the sarsen ring at Stonehenge in order to experience sunrise there in solitude and tranquillity. In that peaceful environment, shortly before dawn, she suddenly heard a 'ringing' sound issuing from a stone close to her. From the information I have from her, it would seem that this is either the sarsen upright numbered 51, or the bluestone num-bered 33 in the north-east section of the site (personal communication and *Erde und Kosmos*, 1985).

22. GLASTONBURY TOR, SOMERSET

Glastonbury is about 35 km (22 miles) south of Bristol, at the meeting of the A39 and A361, between Bath and Taunton. The Tor rises over the town. OS 1:50000 sheet 183. Grid reference: ST 512386.

When approaching Glastonbury, to catch the first glimpse in the distance of the weird, conical hill that is its Tor is a thrill to all but the most unimaginative of souls. It can be seen from considerable distances, rising 159 m (522 ft) above the surrounding landscape. To many it is a spiritual landmark; the classic holy hill.

The Glastonbury region, inhabited since prehistoric times, was composed of islands in a shallow sea until the beginning of the historic era. It became an early Christian centre—with legends of Joseph of Arimathea bringing the Grail there and, even, of Christ having visited the place—and later became associated with King Arthur, the Isle of Avalon. Today it is a mystic focus for various kinds of 'New Age' proponents.

Of the wells around the Tor, the most famous is the chalybeate Chalice Well (which also used to be called the Blood Well because of the red-iron deposits left by its waters) at the foot of the adjacent Chalice Hill. It is a sacred and healing well with origins rooted in distant antiquity—and radioactive (Roberts, 1978).

Strange terraces can be seen on the slopes of the Tor. Some years ago, Geoffrey Russell suggested these to be the remains of a three-dimensional labyrinth that wound its way around the hill, perhaps used in prehistory for initiation rituals. This was a contentious idea at first, but subsequent investigations have shown that a labyrinthine path can indeed be traced around the Tor using these ridges, and consensus opinion is currently that the labyrinth idea could well be correct. It is certainly in keeping with the sense of the hill being sacred from the remotest times. This is also enshrined in the legends of the Tor being the home of Gwynn ap Nudd, the Fairy King as now identified in folklore, but in earlier tradition lord of Annwn (probably the origin of 'Avalon'), the Underworld or Otherworld of spirit.

The symbols of the Christian suppression of this pagan spirituality can be found in folklore and on the Tor itself. In legend, it was supposed to be St Collen who exorcised the old spirit of the hill. Summoned by the Fairy King to a meeting on the summit of the Tor, St Collen secreted a vial of holy water in his robes. On top of the hill, the saint saw a glittering palace, with a banquet laid out within it and sweet music in the air. Instead of accepting the Fairy King's invitation to the magical feast, St Collen threw his holy water over the vision, which went out like a light, and left the saint alone on the dark, windswept hill. On top of the Tor is a tower, the remains of a fourteenth-century chapel dedicated to St Michael, the Christian slayer of the dragon, the symbol to the Christians of evil, and hence of the Elder faiths. But Gwynn ap Nudd obviously still inhabits the deep recesses of the Tor, because an earlier version of St Michael's chapel was destroyed by a thirteenth-century earthquake that shook the Tor.

As might be expected from a place with a tectonic history, Glastonbury Tor, like virtually all holy hills and mountains around the world, attracts light phenomena. I personally witnessed one display in May 1969, while standing near the ruined tower: three balls of orange light emerged out of the blue evening mist gathering around the Tor and made a partial circuit of the western side of the hill before darting away out of sight. Others with me also saw the lights, including a leading Western Buddhist, Sthavira Sangharakshita. Later that same year, four local people saw a disk and a globe of fiery light over the Tor, and in 1970 a police officer reported eight egg-shaped objects, 'dark maroon' in colour, hovering in formation over the hill. In August 1980, a witness saw 'several green and mauve lights hovering around the tower, some smaller than others, about the size of beachballs and footballs. One hovered outside the east-facing window' (Congdon, 1986). On midsummer's day 1981, a group of women on a pilgrimage up the Tor saw a glowing orange form being emitted from St Michael's tower. The atmospheric phenomenon arched through the air and

PLATE 66 Glastonbury Tor.

PLATE 67 Chalice Well, covered with its wood and wrought-iron lid.

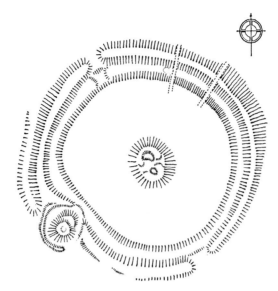

FIG. 20 Plan of the earthworks on Eggardon Hill, depicting the encircling Iron Age banks and ditches and the Bronze Age central barrow remains.

seemed to 'ground' itself near the Chalice Well at the foot of the Tor. One of the witnesses stated that she believed that 'what we saw was the magnetic field' (personal comment).

And so on. There are many accounts of such happenings on this hill of power.

23. EGGARDON HILL, DORSET

Fourteen and a half km (9 miles) west-north-west of Dorchester, alongside a country road running from Askerswell on the A35 to Toller Porcorum to the north. OS 1:50 000 sheet 194. Grid reference: SY 541948.

The hill is crowned with Iron Age earthworks, archaeologically interpreted as a fortified camp. The massive ramparts enclose an area of 8 hectares (20 acres). The major entrance was on the south-east. Hundreds of hollows inside the enclosure are believed to have been storage pits, although very little has been found in them. The hilltop was clearly a sacred place earlier in prehistory, because in the centre of the huge enclosure are the remains of two Bronze Age round barrows.

In September 1974, a motorist on the country road passing the hill saw a bluish ball of light appear in the sky ahead of him, his car engine stalling at the same time. The engine revived after the light had moved off. On the same road in the late 1960s the engines of four cars cut out simultaneously. It took 20 minutes before they could be re-started. Local folklorist Jeremy Harte has noted (1986) that these incidents, reported as real events and documented in the contemporary local press and specialist UFO journals, had become absorbed into local, oral folk-traditions by 1983—hinting at how earlier folklore may well contain elements relating to actual strange experiences at ancient sites.

24. NINE STONES, DORSET

In an enclosure on the south side of the A35 just west of Winterbourne Abbas, 8 km (5 miles) west of Dorchester. OS 1:50 000 sheet 194. Grid reference: SY 610904.

The nine megaliths at this site, known also as the Nine Ladies or the Devil's Nine Stones, form a circle about 8.5 m (28 ft) in diameter. The tallest stone is almost 2.1 m (7 ft) high and weighs approximately 8 tonnes.

Numerous folklore motifs have been attached to the circle. The stones are uncountable; they are the Devil, his wife, and children; they were children turned to stone for playing a game on a Sunday; and they were maidens petrified for dancing on a Sunday. In earlier times, local men would raise their hats when passing the circle, and there was a tradition that the stones danced at 3 pm on certain days.

Jeremy Harte (1986) records an unusual incident alongside the stones:

> On the night of 23rd January 1985, there was a peculiar car breakdown at this site. A breakdown van, towing a damaged Ford Transit, was

PLATE 68 The Nine Stones circle, alongside the A35.

PLATE 69 *Right*: Trethevy Quoit, Cornwall. Note curious hole in corner of capstone, and the missing lower-right portion of front stone.

passing the stones when its engine cut out and the lights of both vehicles failed. A few minutes later the electric circuits of the vehicles (which were not linked) simultaneously came to life again. At the same time (9.15 pm) a similar breakdown occurred on Monkton Hill, when the lights of a Toyota dulled, flashed on and off six or seven times, and then returned to normal.

There are clearly similarities here with the events alongside Eggardon Hill many years earlier. The local press also made this connection.

25.   TRETHEVY QUOIT, CORNWALL

Located 5 km (3 miles) north of Liskeard in a field behind cottages at a junction and sharp bend on the country road linking the hamlets of Tremar and Darite. OS 1:50 000 sheet 201. Grid reference: SX 259688.

'Quoit' is a term often applied to dolmens in Cornwall. This is one of the most impressive in Britain, standing almost 4.5 m (15 ft) at its highest point—well-deserving of its earlier, local name of 'Giant's

House'. Its seven uprights support a huge slab of a capstone 3.7 m (12 ft) long that slopes sharply down to the rear, western, end of the structure. The steepness of the angle has been exaggerated by the collapse of the western support stone, but it would always have sloped. At the highest, north-east corner of the capstone is a curious hole, purpose, if any, unknown. The impressive upright at the front, eastern end of the dolmen has a small hole cut out of its lower right-hand corner, just big enough to admit a body—alive, deceased, or entranced. The dolmen was probably partially surrounded by a mound from which the stone chamber protruded in its pristine state.

The quoit is built of granite, a radioactive rock as mentioned earlier. The enclosed chamber is, therefore, bound to have a high natural radiation count. And so it proves. Measurements taken in July 1988, using three different radiation counters (two running automatically and simultaneously inside the chamber and in the environment for a prolonged timed period, and the other a rapid-count machine employed for multiple, short-timed counts inside and outside the structure) gave a composite reading 103 per cent higher inside the dolmen than in the surroundings.

This quoit is a type of monument referred to in archaeology as a 'portal dolmen'. Portal dolmens usually have an inner chamber sloping towards the rear, as here, and have protruding slabs at the front forming a portal or small forecourt. This area had ritual use and, as archaeologist John Barnatt has written of such sites (1982), 'it seems probable that much of the chamber remained empty and that they never contained a large number of artefacts or burials'. So these things were not simply big graves—they were actively used by the living for some purpose.

26. PENDEEN VAU, CORNWALL

Located in the farmyard of Pendeen Manor Farm on a small road leading to Pendeen lighthouse on the north Penwith coast, off the B3306 between St Just and Morvah (left turn at Higher Boscaswell if going towards Morvah). Seek permission at farm. OS 1:50 000 sheet 203. Grid reference: SW 384355.

This site is a *fogou*, the Cornish term for subterranean stonelined passageways or galleries. They are often called *souterrains* where they occur elsewhere—Ireland, Brittany, north-east Scotland, and the Orkney islands. There has been stiff debate in the past about their function. The orthodox view has been that they were refuges in times of trouble or, the more popular idea, that they were storage places. An alternative view, however, is that they were intended for ritual or ceremonial purposes. There is no direct evidence for any of these views, and it may also be an error to assume all such underground structures as these were intended for the same function in the different regions in which they occur.

The Cornish fogous are dated to the first millennium BC, and are usually located beneath Iron Age villages. The refuge idea for them is almost certainly incorrect, as Ian Cooke (1987) points out:

> you would be entirely at the mercy of anyone who might find your refuge. No provisions were made for an 'escape passage' or for extra ventilation (both features common in Irish souterrains), and a few large boulders laid over the entrance would have buried you and your companions alive, while a fire could have been used to asphyxiate the occupants.

Nor does the storage notion fare much better. Nothing has been uncovered during archaeological investigation at any of these sites to support it, and Cooke also points out (*ibid.*) that 'in wintertime water would be dripping from the roof as gales lashed the earth above. Strange place to use as a larder for perishable foods'.

The likelihood of ritual use being the purpose of these places is now looked on a little more favourably by most people, and the faded carving of a man and serpent at the entrance to the Boleigh fogou (below) seems to hint that may be the correct approach. The new evidence being released in this present book will support this view, and may even give clues as to the nature of the religious activities involved.

I believe the Cornish fogous were yet another structural design created in prehistory to make opportunistic use of the radioactive properties of the environment. And it is interesting to note that most, if not all, of the north-east Scottish souterrains occur in granitic areas— Brittany is granitic, while in Orkney uranium has been found in stream water (Michie and Cooper, 1979). The interior of Pendeen Vau gives a similar radiation reading to Trethevy Quoit (which here registered as 91 per cent higher than the local exterior background) and is identical with the interior of the King's Chamber in Egypt's Great Pyramid (see Part Three).

Pendeen Vau is an exciting site to visit. Its entrance is in one of those immense walls of uncertain antiquity known in Cornwall as 'hedges'. The main passage descends steeply from the entrance, with a litter of loose stones on the floor. After about 6 m (20 ft), the passage turns at a sharp angle to the left, and a longer section disappears into the darkness, punctuated only by the dim light entering through a small hole towards the far end. At the point where the passageway turns, there is a quartz stone embedded in the wall, shining out distinctively. At this point also is a miniature entrance into a smaller chamber that,

PLATE 70   The entrance to Pendeen Vau fogou.

PLATE 71   Looking back along first length of passage towards entrance.

PLATE 72   *Right*: Peering into the eerie darkness of the longest length of passage in the fogou.

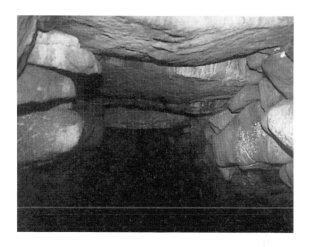

remarkably, has not been lined with stone but merely cut out of the clay and left in its raw state. This condition is known as 'rab cut'.

This mysterious place has had various legends told about it. It was once said that the subterranean passage extended as far as the Scilly Isles or other distant destinations. The fogou was rumoured to possess a treasure. And there was the 'Spirit of Pendeen Vau': a beautiful woman dressed in white who appears at the entrance of the fogou at the winter solstice ('Christmas') with a red rose in her mouth. In another version of the legend, the White Lady turns into a horrific entity if one follows her down into the fogou.

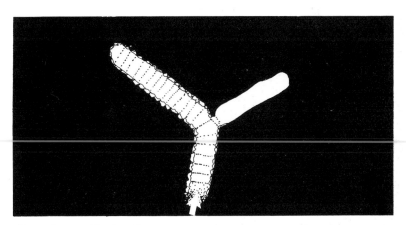

FIG. 21 Layout of Pendeen Vau.

153

27. CHÛN QUOIT, CORNWALL

Situated on open moorland close to the tumbled stones of Chûn Castle, an Iron Age
enclosure. On country road coming from Morvah (on B3306) towards Madron, a
right-hand turn leads to farm below Chûn Castle. Marked footpath from farm to
monuments. OS 1:50 000 sheet 203. Grid reference: SW 402339.

Very well preserved, Chûn Quoit stands impressively on the moor like some megalithic mushroom. The 2.4-m (8-ft) square capstone sits on a virtually complete chamber. The remains of a low mound surround the dolmen, and isolated small uprights and slabs in the vicinity of the quoit may represent the remains of the mound's kerb and a possible entrance forecourt. Structural details on the dolmen suggest that it was never designed to be entirely covered. As so often the case with this type of monument, no bones or artefacts were to be found inside the chamber. A small gap between two of the chamber uprights allow entry to the inside at a squeeze.

In the summer of 1979, archaeologist John Barnatt was engaged in a huge survey of the ceremonial monuments of Cornwall. He and his photographer, Brian Larkman, spent weeks 'in the field'. They had reached Chûn Quoit by 21 July. Something remarkable and extremely

informative happened to the two men there. Here is Barnatt's account published for the first time:

> After spending the afternoon surveying the site we set up camp for the night on moorland a short distance to the south. After supper, as it was a fine clear night, Brian and I returned to the Quoit to have a further look round and just generally relax after a tiring day. We both took a turn at crawling through the gap between side slab and capstone and sitting alone in the interior. Much to our surprise, we each witnessed an inexplicable light phenomenon. When looking up at the undersurface of the capstone, periodic short bursts of multicoloured light (with colours reminiscent of a rainbow) flashed across the stone's surface in short linear bands—this happened intermittently over something like 30 minutes. We both commented to each other at the time and could find no obvious explanation for the effect. It was already dark and the Quoit is located on a hilltop which isolates it from the surrounding landscape; there are no nearby roads or tracks that allow car headlights to have been responsible (in any event the lights were coloured).
>
> (Personal communication)

Larkman's experience was slightly different—and more complex. As he prised himself through the opening into the chamber he saw what he described in his diary at the time as 'a reflection of myself, ghostlike in the shadows of the stone slab opposite'. In 1988, in response to my request for more information on this incident, Larkman attempted to rationalize the image he saw, his 'reflection'. 'Was it a hallucination—perhaps caused by the move from the relative light of the open air to the complete darkness of the tomb?' he asked rhetorically. The figure had seemed 'almost like a retinal image'. But he also saw the lights—'a real phenomenon taking place within the tomb':

> The lights seemed quite simply to be a faint illumination from outside, as if a torch or car headlight was shining from some distance, flickering over the underside of the capstone, showing its irregularities off...This continued for most of the 20 minutes that I stayed inside the tomb. Yet when I climbed out I could see no sign of any lights at all. And there were certainly none to be seen before I climbed in.
>
> (Personal communication)

We will encounter similar lights again in another radioactive environment below.

Chûn Quoit does seem to be built from particularly energetic granite—its internal readings taken in June 1988 were 123 per cent higher than those taken simultaneously in the environment, and the actual counts were 31 per cent higher than even those of Trethevy or Pendeen Vau.

28. MADRON HOLY WELL AND CHAPEL, CORNWALL

Reached by a lane north off the Morvah–Madron–Penzance country road 1 km (1/2 mile) west of Madron, signposted 'Wishing Well'. After a short distance along lane there is a footpath through woods on right for 1/2 km (1/4 mile) to well. OS 1:50 000 sheet 203. Grid reference: SW 447328.

There are not many places more atmospheric than Madron well, its 'Baptistry', and their approach. The footpath through the woods is like a magic, green-hued walk redolent of former times and beliefs. By the time the visitor reaches the turning for the well on the left, the twentieth century seems far away.

A low signboard indicates the general direction to the well, located amidst a tangled copse that, when I visited at least, is a mire underfoot and the stone-lined well difficult to locate. There has apparently been many changes to the form of the well's stonework over the years. A photograph in 1910 shows it surrounded by massive blocks of granite and the well opening rectangular (Leggat, 1987). Today the wellhead is a circular construction of granite. This ancient holy place is still frequented, and votive rags can be found tied to tree branches around the spot.

A hundred metres to the north-east of the well itself is the ruined chapel, sometimes incorrectly referred to as a baptistry. This ruined granite building has been dated to the fourteenth century, but there is a wide body of opinion that dates its foundations to centuries earlier. Roofless, the overhanging foliage gives a green cast to the interior. The spring water is fed into a 'reservoir' in the south-west corner. There is a stone altar on the east wall and a stone bench running round the walls of the small chapel. The very soul of Celtic Christianity, with its powerful Pagan ancestry, seems to be here.

Madron well was famed for both its prophetic, oracular, powers and its healing properties. Healing took place at both the well and the chapel, though it seems as if most took place in the old building. In the 1600s a celebrated and well-documented case of healing took place here, when John Trelille was made able-bodied after being crippled for 16 years. He was bathed in the waters at the chapel once a week for three weeks, after which time he was fully healed, and went on to live an active life as a soldier. Apart from curing cripples, the well was supposed to be especially efficacious in the treatment of skin diseases, colic, shingles, and general aches and pains. It was the tradition for mothers to bring their ailing children to the waters (primarily in the chapel it seems) on the first three Sunday mornings in May. The children were plunged naked three times into the water.

Being granite, the radiation readings in the chapel are of course higher than the exterior background. But I found by floating counters on the water that the water surface gives the highest readings of all, over double that of the environment, and 49 per cent higher than the interior of the chapel.

29. SANCREED HOLY WELL, CORNWALL

Tucked away 1/2 km (1/4 mile) west of the church in Sancreed, 8 km (5 miles) south-east of St Just. An obscure path leads off from the farmyard across the road from the church, and winds northwards to well site. OS 1:50 000 sheet 203. Grid reference: SW 418293.

This is a secret, enchanted place. The well is set in a virtually subterranean stone structure reminiscent of a cavern, down a flight of stone steps. In the half-light of the interior, the water, clear as crystal, can barely be perceived. There is ample room to stand. In the wild garden area surrounding the well are the remnants of a chapel. The headstones of the graves of Juliet Shanks and her husband poke through the undergrowth. On her stone it says, 'she caused this sanctuary to be cleared and kept in a state befitting a holy place'. Sanctuary. Holy place. These are the sort of terms to describe this location.

Little seems to be known or written about Sancreed holy well, though most commentators agree about the exceptional aura of sanctity at the place. The well has been recently signposted, and its access is more apparent than formerly.

The prime energy effect of the place is the sense of calm it engenders. Peace. Repose. I have actually seen every person in a group of 15 people enter a deep, languid state here, or fall completely asleep! It is a place to sleep; to have the Dream of Earth. The waters at Sancreed

PLATE 74 Looking into the roofless old chapel at Madron. In the corner is the reservoir of holy well water, where cures are said to have taken place.

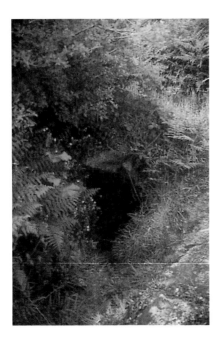

PLATE 75 The mysterious and powerful Sancreed holy well. Stone steps lead down underground to the water from this almost overgrown entrance.

have given me (with their permission) the highest radiation counts I have obtained anywhere in Cornwall, registering here nearly 200 per cent overall above background. With one instrument, in fact, readings off the surface of the water itself were regularly in the order of three times or more those found in the exterior background (and see Fig. 28 in Part Three).

Sleepiness and enhanced natural radiation levels are not, in my view, unconnected—as discussed further in Part Three.

30. CARN EUNY FOGOU, CORNWALL

Located just over 6.5 km (4 miles) west-south-west of Penzance, near the hamlet of Brane. This is on a lane off the Lower Drift (on A30) to Sancreed country road. Foot approach to Carn Euny from car park at Brane. Site is in care of English Heritage, and is signposted. OS 1:50000 sheet 203. Grid reference: SW 402288.

The Iron Age settlement here was rediscovered by chance only last century, with excavations taking place in the 1860s (by Cornish antiquarian Copeland Borlase) and between 1964 and 1974. It seems the site had seen activity from Bronze Age and possibly Neolithic times, but was settled in the middle of the first millennium BC. The community was active until around AD 400, the people being farmers and stockbreeders, with some involvement with the tin trade. The houses had clay floors and stone-covered drainage systems. The community had a grain store in the form of a deep pit lined with china clay (discovered in 1965). The earliest dwellings were timber, and the 'beehive hut' and fogou were the first stone structures at the place— seemingly pre-dating permanent houses at the site.

The now roofless beehive hut, 4.6 m (15 ft) in diameter, was built first (around 500 BC), and is unique in Cornwall. It had a corbelled structure, with the walls below ground level and a short entrance passage. A century or two later the fogou passage or gallery was built. This was roofed over with massive granite blocks and was over 20 m (65 ft) in length. It remains intact, with about 12.8 m (42 ft) of it still roofed. Although now open at both ends, the 2 m (6.5 ft) high gallery was originally sealed, and the only access was by means of a tiny 'creep', steeply angled to the surface from the northern side of the gallery's south-west end. Now with just a damp clay floor, when uncovered the fogou was paved with large granite blocks beneath which, in the centre, ran a gutter.

Carn Euny effectively does away with both the refuge and storage explanations for Cornish fogous. It could never have been a hiding

PLATE 76   The now roofless beehive chamber at Carn Euny, the first stone structure at the site.

FIG. 22 Layout of Carn Euny fogou.

PLATE 77 One of the present-day entrances to the fogou. Passageway in foreground has lost its roofing stones.

PLATE 78 Interior of the surviving roofed section of the fogou.

place, because the upper course or two of the walling, and the roof, stood proud of the ground's surface. And the facts that the village had a separate grain store and the creep access was so restrictive, fatally challenge any idea of the fogou being for storage purposes.

Carn Euny fogou has high levels, in natural terms, of internal radioactivity, and this despite its ends being open and the granite flooring now removed. In its pristine condition it must have been quite 'hot'! The background at Carn Euny is high in itself, but the fogou during our monitoring registered about 87 per cent higher.

31. BOLEIGH FOGOU, CORNWALL

In the private grounds of Rosemerryn House, which is along a driveway off the northerly side of the B3315, 8 km (5 miles) south-west of Penzance. Permission must be obtained to view the fogou. OS 1:50 000 sheet 203. Grid reference: SW 437252.

The fogou, set into the ramparts of an Iron Age enclosure of which only traces now survive, has an entrance at the south-west and a

PLATE 79 The entrance to Boleigh fogou.

passage 12.2 m (40 ft) long, 1.5 m (5 ft) wide, and over 1.8 m (6 ft) high. On its westernmost side, a short way into the gallery, is a creep with a sharp angle southwards along its passage and an airshaft hole in the roof. A stone on the left as one enters the fogou has a profoundly indistinct carving, first noted by Dr E.B. Ford during his excavations of the fogou in 1957. Ford described (cited in Clark, 1961) infra-red pictures of it as showing

> A male figure, apparently full-faced, with long hair around the head, the left side of the face being flecked away. The right arm, raised from the elbow, supports a spear; the left is held horizontally to the elbow, the forearm being lifted vertically, the hand grasping a lozenge-shaped object...possibly the head of a serpent, one of the coils of which being dimly suggested around the wrist...
>
> If, as is possible, the figure symbolizes a Celtic or Roman-British deity [it] might represent [the fogou's] presiding genius, thus establishing a unique function for the building as a temple for the religious use of the occupants of the fort.

Ford's excavations revealed ten pieces of Iron Age pottery—some of it patterned—from within the fogou, and a rock-cut shelf at the far end of

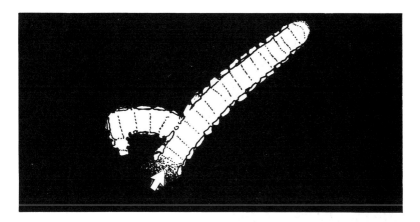

Fig. 23   Layout of Boleigh fogou.

the main passage, which may possibly have served as a shrine or altar.

Rosemerryn House and grounds now form the Centre for Alternative Education and Research (CAER), and its director is Jo May, a former research psychologist at the University of Sussex. CAER uses an idealization of the fogou carving as its logo, and May feels it could represent Clew an Nemed ('Clew of the Sanctuary'), a Celtic god of healing—similar carvings are found in Brittany. (Some of the pottery found at Carn Euny was thought to have Breton origin, illustrating the undoubted links between the two lands in the Iron Age.)

Fig. 24   Idealized version of the Boleigh carving incorporated in the CAER logo.

Because of the courses CAER runs, many people have a chance to experience the fogou quietly, intimately, and over a period of time, and it is used for meditation, ceremony, and research. It thus gets a use and observation denied the other remaining fogous. Various experiences in the fogou have been reported by people. May says these claims range through recurring visions (with different people) of 'women in white', inner voices, a stilling of inner turmoil, senses of symbolic death and rebirth, and so on. There is also a definite physical, body effect: after a few minutes of being inside the fogou, body temperature rises a degree or two, irrespective of air temperature.

Something else happened in June 1988, though. Quite spontaneously, Jo May told my wife and I about it when we visited the fogou on 1 July in order to monitor its radiation. Some weeks earlier, a group of Amerindians had visited CAER, and had noted that the fogou was very similar to the Pueblo Indian subterranean ritual chambers known as *kivas*. They conducted a *kiva* dance in the fogou. One of them suggested

PLATE 80   The third millennium BC granite chamber of Gavrinis, Brittany, probably would have produced light phenomena like Boleigh or Chûn Quoit. Jo May describes some of the lights as 'whorls' looking like fingerprints . . . similar designs are carved into some of the Gavrinis stones.

to May that he ought to spend a whole night in the structure. Realizing that he had lived with the fogou for ten years but had never stayed a night in it, May thought it was time he did so. On 19 June, he settled into the main passage, and did not sleep or use a light source of any kind all night. This is what he experienced:

> Just at the point of dawn, as light was beginning to break, I saw thin spirallic filaments swirling in front of my eyes and around the main capping lintels of the passage. At first I thought it was a retinal image (much like 'floaters' or dead cells on the eyeball). But I had never experienced such spirallic phenomena before and they seemed to be moving independently of my eye movements. They most closely resembled the whorls on fingertips, but lots of them, interlaced and moving gently.
>
> Then I saw hundreds of tiny pricks of light, like stars, again moving gently, with the occasional streak as if some of them were shooting stars.
>
> I checked that this was not some kind of subjective or self-produced effect by switching my gaze back to the emerging light at the entrance of the fogou, and then redirecting my gaze at several points within the passage.
>
> The stars returned unmistakably.
>
> The whole passage appeared to be filled with what can best be described as a star soup which flowed in and around the stones.
>
> Somehow, I 'knew' that what I was seeing was energy, which, although subtle, was clearly 'there'. I suspect that the ability to see it depends on certain fine tuning of perception which is probably available to anyone.
>
> (Personal communication)

There was no way, of course, that May could have any idea of the Chûn Quoit experiences privately related to me long before by Dr John Barnatt and Brian Larkman.

I feel confident that we are hearing now, for the first time, of a light phenomenon associated with enclosures possessing certain levels of natural radioactivity. And Boleigh fogou is energetic: its actual readings are even higher than Chûn Quoit, though a little less than Sancreed holy well, by our measurements; its relative level is double that of the (high) exterior-background levels at Rosemerryn. The site had been monitored for the Dragon Project in 1983 by Alan Bleakley, and his findings also confirmed the relatively high counts of the fogou's interior.

6 OTHER SITES

Numerous other sites have been investigated with regard to energy effects, or have come to notice because of a story of interest attached to them. These encounters have produced mixed results—interesting findings, unexpected happenings, revealing histories, confusing or negative results—and so to complete this section on sites, I provide here a brief but representative selection of such cases.

CORNISH CIRCLES AND RADIATION

Some of Cornwall's stone circles have been subject to radiation monitoring because of Cornwall's interesting levels of background radiation, but findings have been contradictory. Readings for the Dragon Project were taken at selected circles and background-control

PLATE 81 Boskednan circle, Cornwall.

locations by Alan Bleakley in 1982. The results at first seemed to indicate a fascinating pattern of *lower*-than-background radiation values in the stone rings. Bleakley's readings at the Boskednan, or Nine Maidens, circle (at SW 434351 on open moorland near Ding Dong Mine) produced a count near the centre of the ring of 12 cpm on a machine that was giving an average Cornish-background reading of 30 cpm. Furthermore, on the three subsequent monitoring sessions at Boskednan, the site average has always been below that of its surroundings. With granite stones forming the ring, one would expect the readings to be higher if anything.

At the Stannon circle (at SX 125801 on Bodmin Moor), Bleakley was amazed to find that his geiger counter was silent for a prolonged period of time. He was able to confirm that it was not instrument failure, and that readings could be obtained at some distance in the countryside around. Theoretically, there always has to be *some* background radiation, however moderate. This anomaly was never explained. When successful monitoring did resume at the circle, though, results matched those for the background.

While a few other monitoring sessions showed some Cornish circles also tended towards lower-than-background readings, or at least to have puzzling long gaps between counts, there were to be no neat patterns. For example, the Merry Maidens circle (at SW 432245 alongside the B3315 near Boleigh) gave paradoxical results. The first monitoring session in 1982 gave readings within this well-preserved ring much higher than any obtained in its surroundings, yet when Don Robins monitored the site in 1985 he found that geiger readings approximately halved when he moved inside the circle of stones. A monitoring session in 1988 showed a site average at the Merry Maidens a little below that of the environment, but of no great significance.

A SOLSTITIAL ENIGMA

In Scotland, the main Callanish site (Callanish I) gave a curious radiation result in 1983. Gaia Programme monitor G. Ronald Curtis and his small team conducted extensive readings between 20 and 24 June (over the solstitial period) at the Callanish group of sites. Callanish I was monitored on both 20 and 24 June. On the first session, the site-average radiation reading and that of its surroundings gave closely matching results, but on 24 June the site average registered as 32 per cent higher than its background. Over the two sessions most of the stones comprising the site gave consistent readings, but certain megaliths roughly doubled their count on 24 June. It is difficult to

PLATE 82   The cruciform setting of stones at Callanish I rise out of the peat like broken teeth. The tall central stone has both hornblende and feldspar embedded in it.

account for variations of this magnitude, and the question as to whether the solstice was in any way a factor remains unresolved.

GAIA PROGRAMME

When the results of the Gaia Programme were processed in 1988, no sign of any consistent pattern showed up, but two histograms (Fig. 25) produced from the findings do show a distinct difference between circle readings and those taken at 'dummy' or randomly selected control sites.

The procedure for taking readings at both actual and control sites and their environments was always identical. Every column on the histogram has resulted from around 40–50 individual readings totalling hours of actual monitoring time. The vertical scale on both histograms is the same, allowing direct comparison. Volunteer monitors on the programme were asked to do at least one dummy site per region in which actual sites were monitored, plus a few regions where there are no megaliths (such as East Anglia). In the event, only seven of these were done. But they are enough to compare with the 25 stone circles monitored during the programme.

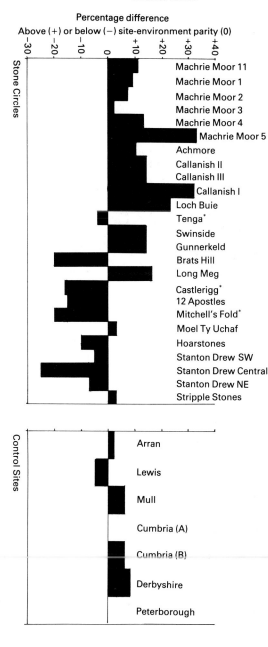

FIG. 25 Histograms allowing comparison of averaged radiation counts between the 25 stone circles and the seven control locations monitored on the Gaia Programme, expressed in percentage terms above or below their respective averaged background readings. See text. The three stone circles asterisked are ones known to possess stones that strongly affect compasses—it is possibly noteworthy that they are all sites with radiation averages below that of their environments. (Most of the sites here have not yet been checked for compass anomalies.)

The two histograms show the site-to-environment relationships for, respectively, the actual sites and the control locations, in terms of percentage differences. If site and surroundings gave the same average radiation readings, there is no column—the difference being zero; the greater the difference between site and surroundings, the longer the column is, either above or below the centre-zero line on the histograms depending on whether the site had higher or lower readings than the environment. It can be seen that out of all the sites, only two control sites (Cumbria A and Peterborough) came out the same for site and environment. This is of course the classic control result: a difference in readings is ideally not expected. Indeed, the largest percentage difference between the values for the dummy sites compared with their environments was 8 per cent. By contrast, the actual stone-circle sites differed up to 33 per cent from their environments, and none of them precisely matched its environment. The range of variation around the zero line is markedly greater for the actual sites than for the control locations.

While this suggests a difference between many real sites compared with control sites, it yields no clue as to any meaningful pattern, with some sites being above background levels, some below, and a few within the same margins as the control sites.

Taken altogether, the picture of radiation at stone-circle sites remains confused. Sometimes there has seemed to be a trend, but either it has dissolved in front of our eyes, or the resource restrictions on this volunteer, unorthodox work has prevented a possible pattern being properly followed up. It may be that whatever variations are perceived are due simply to random fluctuations in background radiation levels or, alternatively, that complex radiation cycles or behaviour patterns are sporadically in play and are in some way modified in the presence of megalithic groupings. We will never know for sure until large numbers of sites can be continuously monitored for very long periods.

AT EASTER AQUORTHIES

The nearest we have so far come to such a situation was in a unique radiation-monitoring experiment carried out by Cosimo and Ann Favaloro at Easter Aquorthies, a 19.5-m (64-ft) diameter recumbent stone circle in north-east Scotland (NJ 732208).

A recumbent circle is one with a stone in its circumference lying flat, often appearing like a massive altar flanked by two uprights. There are a large number of these sites in north-east Scotland, and there have been archaeological suggestions that some of them might be aligned to the moon at the point in its 18.6-year cycle known as the 'major lunar standstill'. In the year of a major lunar standstill, the winter full-moonrise will reach its northernmost position, and in the same year the summer full-moonrise will reach its southernmost point. The height of the moon's journey across the sky in such a year also varies dramatically: to the observer the moon can arc high overhead one month, and be seen skimming the horizon during another. Prehistorian Aubrey Burl feels that some of the recumbent circles may have related to these extreme lunar positions for ceremonial effect; so, for example, a major standstill-period low moon might seem to 'roll' across the (often perfectly horizontal) surface of the recumbent stone at some circles. Burl suggested (1987) Easter Aquorthies as one of the recumbent sites having probable major lunar-standstill significance. 1987 was a major lunar-standstill year, and 29 September was one of the important dates of that year (a moonset), so that was when the Favaloros arranged to be at the site.

They conducted both instrumental and human-response experiments, but here we need consider only their radiation monitoring. They used two Dragon Project instruments specially designed to monitor background radiation and that kept automatic counts. One was positioned inside the circle, the other was placed at a point at a distance in the environment. The two instruments were run simultaneously, and readings taken from them simultaneously at 15-minute intervals over an almost 12-hour period, from 3.45 pm on 29 September to 2.45 am the next morning. The moon set at 9 pm, so the monitoring period 'bracketed' the event by several hours. Not only did this experiment represent the longest continuous period of simultaneous site-and-environment radiation monitoring so far undertaken, it was utterly unique in that the period covered such a significant lunar event.

We can see the outcome in Fig. 26. Two remarkable things are indicated. The first is that at 4.30 pm on 29 September, there was an extraordinary flare-up of readings at the site while the environment remained normal. This increase was of considerable magnitude as can be seen, and demonstrates clearly that radiation levels can change at a site while the surroundings are not affected. On this basis, the odd fluctuations we have noted at Rollright and some of the other circles referred to above might have been site related after all, and therefore significant from an energy-effect perspective.

The rest of the graph shows that through almost the entire period, the site (solid line) registered higher readings than the surroundings (broken line), the two sets of measurements meeting at only three points. The longest and major one of these points of contact, however, occurred *precisely over the moonset period*, and it was only then when the background readings twice edged above those of the site. For this to have happened only at this time during the course of 12 hours makes it difficult to dismiss as merely coincidence.

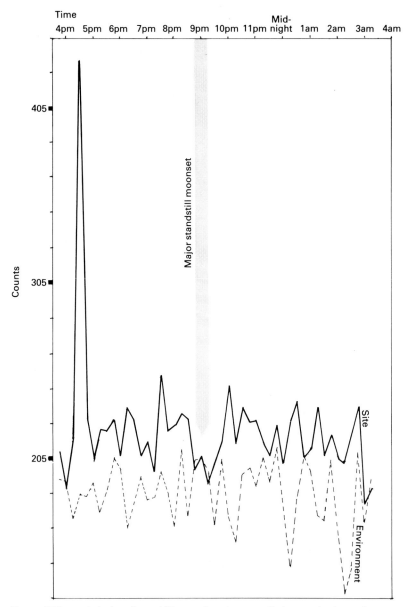

Fig. 26 This graph depicts almost 12 hours of continuous radiation monitoring at the Easter Aquorthies site (solid bold line) simultaneous with its environment (broken line). The dramatic flare-up of readings at the site is clearly visible, as is the period of overlap of the two sets of readings at the time of moonset. See text for further discussion [*After Favaloro*].

Finally, it can be seen that for most of the period there was a tendency, though obviously not an exact pattern, for site readings to increase around the times the background readings were decreasing (Favaloro and Favaloro, personal communication and data). These results should give everyone interested in ancient sites, from whatever viewpoint, food for thought.

SOUNDINGS

Apart from radiation work, there have been numerous other fragments of research, information, and observation. For instance, the search for radio anomalies such as those noted at Rollright has so far produced only one other location where the curious 'cubes' of signal propagation have been noted—using Rodney Hales' special wide-band radio receiver, I picked up the bizarre signals at several places amongst ruined Bronze Age cairns atop the hill overlooking Baltinglass, in the Wicklow Hills, Ireland. The signal would occur in highly localized areas about 60 cm (2 ft) across. These were mostly within recesses within the megalithic ruins. Ironically, I could not detect the signals in exposed positions on the hilltop where one would normally expect radio reception.

I tested this site because of an anecdote passed on to me by the artist, Chris Castle: in 1974 he had been studying the Wicklow site and had heard a curious humming noise. Investigation confirmed that the sound was originating from within the recesses of a cairn. Castle could find no explanation for it. This was just one of a number of reported

PLATE 83 Bronze Age cairns surrounded by Iron Age walling in the Wicklows, near Baltinglass, Ireland.

instances where sound has been reported at or around sites. (This aspect might relate to the apparent ultrasound.) The incident at Stonehenge has already been mentioned in the guide, but there are other cases. On the midsummer solstice, 1987, Michael Woolf and Rachel Garcia visited the 3.3-m (11-ft) tall Cornish monolith called the Blind Fiddler, close beside the Penzance to Sennen A30 road. At the precise moment the sun set, they heard 'a sudden, muffled thunderclap, audible but emanating from beneath the earth'. It did not shake the ground but seemed to alter the air pressure (Woolf and Garcia, 1977). Another area associated with anomalous sound is that around Arthur's Stone, a dolmen on the Herefordshire–Wales border (SO 318431) close to the village of Dorstone. After a severe thunderstorm one evening in 1978, villagers could hear a peculiar faint high-pitched buzzing sound that was never identified. Researcher S.L. Birchby observes (1987): 'Records of sounds heard on the hills of Wiltshire, Sussex, Wales and places more distant from modern history—but all with prehistoric remains—indicate something strange and unexplored'.

LIGHTS AND SITES

As with sounds, so with lights. Specific sites and light events have been described above, in the guide, but this represents the tip of an iceberg that awaits to be uncovered. Folklore teems with stories of fairies and prehistoric sites, and in many cases these 'fairies' turn out to be lights—as the very term 'fairy lights' suggests. Some folklore items, though, refer to actual events that were not clothed in the cloak of legend (as we noted could happen even in modern times with the

PLATE 84 *Left*: The author picking up anomalous radio signals at the Baltinglass cairns [*John Steele*].

PLATE 85 The Blind Fiddler monolith, Cornwall.

Eggardon Hill occurrences). During the nineteenth century, for example, a cairn near Torhousemuir, west of Wigtown, Scotland, produced a wandering light on several evenings that was witnessed by numerous local people (Grinsell, 1976). Again, it was reported in 1885 that for a limited period, miners returning from their work at night repeatedly saw lights 'on and around' the complex Bronze Age barrow of Carn Gluze, on the coastal cliffs at St Just, Cornwall. In this case the lights did become associated with fairies. In Scotland once more, on the Island of Bute, Carn Bhan (NS 006693) was known locally as a place of 'apparitions', but McLagen, writing in *Folklore* in 1893, was able to interview a 70-year-old local woman who informed him that 'there used to be a large light often seen at the Carn Bhan, indeed I think it is not so very long ago since it was seen there. I have often seen it myself there, it was as large as the light of that lamp'.

The guide has already indicated moorlands containing concentrations of prehistoric sites that are the foci of light phenomena. This sort of association will be extended as more information becomes available about the geographical zones that particularly harbour earth lights. So, for instance, it has recently been discovered that an area of central Wales around the Elan Valley and Hafren Forest—between Llanidloes and Devil's Bridge—has been the source of light phenomena for as long as some local people can recall. This is a wild, largely uninhabited part of Wales that relatively few people in Britain know exists. An upsurge in the incidence of light phenomena in the autumn of 1987 brought the area and the lights to the attention of a wider public. Light phenomena were being seen flashing off the tops of the hills in the region, and deep, rumbling subterranean sounds were also heard. People relatively new to the area were worried that these events were 'something to do' with the presence of a secret research unit of British Aerospace in Hafren Forest, but investigations have now clearly shown that occasional appearances of such lights have occurred throughout the lifetimes of some of the indigenous inhabitants of the region (Devereux, 1989). The lights emerge from the summits of the hills and mountains in the form of purple-white flashes and (further west) as globes of blue light. These same summits are extensively punctuated with prehistoric cairns, and one wonders if the area was attractive to the cairn builders because of the visible, luminescent spirits of the hills (or of the Dead haunting the peaks). It is worth recalling that the association of cairns with lights was so well-known that the Scandinavians had the term '*haug-eldir*' (Part One) to describe it.

Such possibilities might supply totally unexpected explanations for odd items of fairy folklore. An example of this is perhaps to be found at the circle (SK 215868) on Hordron Edge, Derbyshire, overlooking the Derwent Valley. A particular stone in this ten-stone, 16-m (53-ft) diameter circle is associated with fairies, and it was the custom to leave milk on it as a gift to them. Why that stone? Why fairies? John Barnatt (1978) has written: 'the stone circle builders not only used the landscape around them for astronomical foresights, but had an interest in its intrinsic nature'. I think the Hordron fairy stone may relate to an aspect of the 'intrinsic nature' of this location. This stone is on the side of the circle pointing towards the rugged Peak District. Three peaks dominate the horizon behind the stone—Win Hill, Mam Tor (itself the location of Bronze Age and Iron Age remains), and Kinder Scout. We now know because of the work of Project Pennine that this area, *and these peaks in particular*, sporadically produce light phenomena that have been widely witnessed and recorded by the most reliable and capable of observers in modern times. Moreover, some of the people living out in those wilds have reluctantly admitted that they and their parents

PLATE 86 The 'Fairy Stone' in the Hordron Edge stone circle. On the skyline the peaks of Win Hill (left) and Mam Tor (right) can be seen, with the bulk of Kinder Scout in distance at right. All these heights have had light phenomena reported around them.

before them have seen these lights from time to time, and are an accepted (if slightly feared) part of the environment.

We are in the ridiculous position of light phenomena occurring with some regularity in certain localized regions of the landscape (some of these can now be specifically identified in Britain, the USA, Scandinavia, India and elsewhere), but to the indigenous inhabitants in such areas, the lights are just part of the local scene, nothing to get excited about. And the locals are generally unwilling to talk to 'outsiders' about the lights, anyway. On the 'outside' we have orthodox science that, on the whole, does not accept or believe in such phenomena. It says they do not exist. Archaeologists come out of this milieu, and so they can hardly be expected to look for an association between sites and lights. Even folklorists have failed to realize that there is a specific category of lore that needs to be filed under 'L' for 'Lights'. Occasionally, when there is an upsurge of earth lights for a short period, we have a 'UFO flap', and that brings out the ufologists. Ufology is considered lunatic fringe by the orthodoxy, which further exacerbates existing prejudices. To be sure, most ufology is lunatic fringe—though a limited handful of UFO investigators show more balanced objectivity than many professional scientists.

So between them all—the locals, the scientists, and the lunatic fringe—the phenomenon continues to be relegated to the night of our ignorance. But in the prehistoric night things would have been different. In such times, when skies were actually seen, and the night truly experienced, these lights would have been perceived. And thought about. And incorporated into the going cosmology of the day.

ON-SITE OBSERVATIONS

Finally, a few of the odd and unexpected observations made by investigators at sites ought to be put on record. Although seemingly tangential, they may hold clues regarding anomalous energy research.

It was noticed during the early years of the Dragon Project that those workers with quartz timepieces who were exposed to the Rollright circle for the longest periods experienced problems with them, whether wristwatches or clocks. They would simply stop functioning. Though it became something of a joke among project volunteers, the phenomenon was never explained.

PLATE 87   The disorienting Altarnun circle, Bodmin Moor.

On his first radiation monitoring session at the Boskednan stone circle (above), Alan Bleakley was caught in a thunderstorm while taking environmental readings. As the electrical storm developed, the geiger readings fell dramatically. Presumably the electrical conditions in the atmosphere were somehow suppressing the cosmic ray component of the background radiation. It is a mechanism that needs to be better understood.

While surveying the Nine Stones or Altarnun circle (SX 236781) on Bodmin Moor, John Barnatt was occasionally interrupted by groups of Royal Marines on an orienteering and route march exercise coming up to the site, taking compass bearings, then departing. Barnatt recalls:

> As I observed them using maps and compass to work out their next destination, I gradually noticed that they frequently set off on strange headings—often 60 degrees out of line. I put this down to their inability to read maps. Later in the day I mentioned this in conversation with one of the officers who were supervising the exercise when he happened to call at the site. He told me that they had chosen the stone circles because in the past they had observed magnetic anomalies at these, which created an added test of the cadets' ability to read maps! As I was using a theodolite to check bearings but had no compass I had no opportunity to check this for myself.
>
> (Personal communication)

In 1988 I briefly tested the stones at this circle for compass effects. None was found, but I did not have time to check if the site as a whole was upsetting specific compass-bearings.

The Stannon stone circle, also on Bodmin Moor, had yielded an anomaly with the periodicity of radiation readings (above), but the readings themselves were quite normal. A partial check for compass anomalies likewise proved fruitless. But the site may hold some deep secrets. While engaged on the mammoth survey of Cornish sites with Barnatt in the Summer of 1979, Brian Larkman recalls that during the periods they camped near the site they observed curious behaviour by the semi-wild moorland ponies:

> On a number of occasions. . .we observed that a relatively large number of the group (20 to 30 animals) spent a large part of the night-time sheltering in the centre of Stannon stone circle. The creatures who stayed in the circle seemed to be predominantly mares and foals, the stallions seeming to prefer to roam around the moor close to the circle.
>
> The stones of the circle are quite small (one to four feet) and offer very little real shelter, and the area of the moor in which the site is situated seems to have no distinctive physical feature to explain why the horses should prefer to spend so much time there.
>
> (Personal communication)

PLATE 88   Stannon stone circle, place of the 'pony ritual'.

Compass, magnetometer, and geiger counter tests conducted by my wife and I at the stone row complexes of Drizzlecombe (from where light phenomena were observed in 1982) and Shovel Down on Dartmoor in May 1988, provided no convincing evidence of unusual energy effects. But while our instruments may have told us nothing, our bodies did. On repeated occasions, we would climb out onto the moor, with heavy backpacks and spend long days hard at work. Yet it was simply a fact that as we left the moor at the end of each day, we both independently noticed that we felt invigorated and charged with energy—against all common sense. We strode off the moor decidedly more energetic than when we had commenced in the mornings! I had a vaguely similar experience many years ago when studying the very long stone row on Ugborough Moor on the southern reaches of Dartmoor. Tracking across difficult terrain with a substantial backpack, I suddenly 'switched' into a much faster rhythm of walking, covering great strides with absolute ease, breathing as calmly as if I were seated in a chair. This was not 'second wind' that I have often experienced in fieldwork, but a distinctive state that verged on the paranormal. I imagine it was something similar to the trance walking called in Tibet, *lung gom*.

How many other visitors who spend any length of time at the Dartmoor stone-row complexes have had similar experiences? I suppose even if they have there is not an accepted context in our society for such experiences to be discussed. Such an experience is just 'one of those things'. Nevertheless, the antiquary, S. Baring-Gould, in his *A Book of Dartmoor* (1900), did make special mention of what he called the 'salubrity' of the moor, noting that it had become 'a thing not unusual' during his day for those suffering from 'delicacy of the lungs' to stay on a farm or cottage on the moor. He also recorded that a physician at Dartmoor Prison remarked in a report in the early 1800s that the exceptionally good health of the prisoners was an 'anomaly', defying the appalling prison conditions and the 'cheerless and hyperborean' moor. Perhaps it all has something to do with the great granite mass that comprises the moor!

There are numerous other anecdotes and research findings that

PLATE 89 Stone rows meet on Shovel Down, Dartmoor.

could be mentioned, but enough has been given in this section to show that there appear to be both definite and as yet less certainly identifiable energy characteristics related to specific classes of ancient sites in Britain. Let us now see if we can begin to make sense of at least two or three of the major measurable or observable effects, and relate them, where appropriate, to sites elsewhere in the world to show that we are dealing with what were universal human interactions with aspects of the natural world.

PART THREE

BREAKING NEW GROUND: PATTERNS, POSSIBILITIES, CONNECTIONS

7 THE PHYSICS OF SHAMANISM

The intimate knowledge the megalith builders had of the nature and character of stone was of a level we can barely guess at today. Egyptologist John Anthony West, gives us an inkling of this knowledge (1985), when discussing a fallen obelisk in the great temple complex of Karnak in Luxor:

> South of the standing obelisk lies its fallen companion, also made of a single block of granite. Though broken, its pointed end still comprises an immense block. Here an interesting test can be performed. Put your ear to the angle of the pyramidion and hit the obelisk with your hand. The entire enormous block resonates like a tuning fork at the slightest blow. This property is undoubtedly a fortuitous result, an inherent property of

PLATE 90 A standing obelisk made of a single piece of granite at the Karnak temple complex, Luxor, Egypt.

PLATE 91 *Right*: The magnetic serpentine outcrop and Indian power-point on Mount Tamalpais, California. The big stone forms a perfect 'seat'.

granite when cut to an obelisk shape. Nevertheless, the resonance itself may well have a deliberate significance...by virtue of their geometry, proportions and measurements, as well as by the careful choice of materials employed, Egyptian temples conform quite literally to Goethe's definition of architecture as 'frozen music'.

West points out that the Egyptian obelisks had very precise dimensions related to very definite and accurate geodetic functions, and were undoubtedly 'scientific' even if they also served as commemorative monuments. Unfortunately, none of the pairs of obelisks used for this purpose are now in position. 'If they were,' he suggests, 'it might have been possible to test for minute alterations in the local magnetic or electrical field with modern equipment' (*ibid.*).

If an individual megalithic block, an outcrop of rock, or a particular type of stone had special properties, including those we today label as 'magnetism' and 'radiation', they would have been known about. This is shown, for example, by an outcrop of serpentine on Mount Tamalpais, which rises to the north of San Francisco. This outcrop, identified by the Indians as one of the power spots on the mountain, is strongly magnetic, as I discovered in 1986. Even small fragments will greatly disturb a compass needle.

TRADITIONAL VIEWS OF POWER STONES

People in early societies would, of course, have pictured these forces in

stone in ways quite different to today's impersonal scientific manner of thinking. These images, or symbolic explanations, would doubtlessly have varied from one society to another. Most are lost to us, but vestiges remain. We can recall, for instance, the Australian aborigine flaking pieces off a boulder to release the *kurunba*, as described in Part One. Some commentators believe that the ancient Egyptians thought of limestone as representing the material, physical world, while radioactive granite symbolized the spiritual (Lemesurier, 1977). Granite was certainly transported great distances in Egypt for specific ceremonial and monumental roles at temple sites (see below).

Certain stones contain spirits, according to the natives of New Guinea, and are called *soimi* stones:

> From each *soimi* stone there emanate certain powerful influences which correspond with those of the spirit-being (*uaropo*) intimately dwelling within it. These forces, whether for the benefit of individuals or the community as a whole, the people seek to turn to profit and advantage.
>
> (Wirtz, cited in Lévy-Bruhl, 1935)

And there must be many more examples of how people saw power in stone. But in whatever form it was culturally perceived, how would radioactivity or magnetism in a stone have been detected by early peoples? And what would those properties of stone have been utilized for?

Each force probably requires different answers, or answers with different emphases, to those questions. Let us look first of all at the matter of ionizing radiation.

RESPONSE TO RADIOACTIVITY

Modern science states that 'ionising radiation cannot be directly detected by the human senses'(NRPB, 1988). This may be true for the five senses as such, but it seems that living organisms do have biological means of being aware of radiation. There are a few fragments of research and experience that relate to this as yet poorly understood area.

A Russian documentary film shown by 'Panorama' (BBC1 TV, 1987), made a passing but telling reference to the behaviour of birds in a town close to the Chernobyl nuclear-power plant immediately after the disaster there had occurred. As if they could literally sense the invisible menace of radiation in the air, *all the birds left*.

Author and researcher Lyall Watson has described (1974) work of the early 1960s that shows that humble creatures like worms can sense radiation:

Frank Brown has tested his planarian worms for response to a very weak gamma radiation emitted by a sample of cesium 137. He found that worms were aware of the radiation and turned away from it, but only when they were moving north or south. They ignored the radiation, no matter where it came from, if they were swimming in any other direction. This shows that gamma rays can be a vector force that somehow indicates direction as well as intensity.

Plants also, it seems, can sense radioactivity. It has been noted in the Scilly Isles (and doubtlessly elsewhere) that bulbs planted near large granite boulders flower early. Presumably radiation from the rock is somehow encouraging their development.

If other living things can sense or react to radiation, perhaps human beings also possess biological means that subtly inform the central nervous system of radiation levels. If so, the old shamans may have been able to develop such an ability and directly sense energy from some stones. This may have been a factor in a shaman's selection of a vision cave or other special place.

Czech-born scientist, Dr Zaboj V. Harvalik has carried out many controlled tests in America with dowsers and is convinced that some skilled dowsers could be more sensitive to weak amounts of radio-activity than geiger counters. Repeated observations by countless generations in ancient times may have indicated the effects had by certain stones or types of rock on the mind and body. These would not only have been ways of noticing the presence of radiation, but would have become the actual reasons for using it and augmenting it in specialized structures.

Radiation is inherently harmful to living tissue. Long exposure to high levels of natural radioactivity can cause illness. In 1972, J. Stängle, a German geobiologist, was able to show with his own gamma-ray detector that certain points in Vilsbiburg, Bavaria, had small areas of high gamma-radiation. He was sure that these peaks in readings were due to the passage of underground water because of hundreds of previous tests and drillings for water at similar points elsewhere. Of interest here was that these zones in Vilsbiburg had been identified 40 years earlier by a dowser as 'geopathological zones'— people living over them had developed cancers.

HEALING

But perhaps homeopathic doses of radiation, as it were, could have *curative* effects. (As the sixteenth-century alchemist Paracelsus put it: 'The poison is the dose'.) This seems to be the case in Boulder,

Montana, USA, where old gold and uranium mines are now being used for giving sufferers of certain ailments strictly timed periods of exposure to the radon concentrations in the abandoned workings. There are claims that the radon atmosphere has helped in cases of arthritis and the control of blood sugar in diabetics, amongst other illnesses. Orthodox medicine challenges such claims, naturally. But one woman user of the radon environment provided by the mines stated that she has been able to dispense with the wheelchair she had to use, and can now happily walk up and down the mine level while she is being exposed to her timed dose of radon (CNN, 1987). Decades ago in America, 'radon kits' were sold for healing purposes, with radon being contained in canisters from which the purchaser could take supposedly healthful sniffs. At the beginning of this century, radioactive caves in Colorado were used for health visits by some Americans in just the same way that their European counterparts would visit spas. But perhaps the two activities were not so dissimilar, if one thinks of the radioactive status of the ancient baths at Bath (Part Two)! The apparent use of Dartmoor at the turn of the century by consumptives, and the effects of the moor's 'salubrity' (Part Two), may possibly be related to the radiation environment of the granite moor with its high-background radiation levels and radon emissions.

If certain levels of, or exposure to, natural radiation can stimulate healing in certain types of disorder, healing traditions connected with particular standing stones could perhaps be explained. For instance, Men an Tol (Part One), where a sick child was passed a number of times through the stone's hole, happens to have a radiation level around the inside edges of the hole about double that of the environment. Could a ring of this energy around a small body really have any effect? Our modern science would dismiss it out of hand—but, then, homeopathy is hardly understood by our orthodox medicine as it is, let alone a more bizarre interaction such as this.

A SLEEP OF POWER

It seems as if a sleepy response can ensue from enhanced natural radioactivity in some instances. I mentioned earlier, for example, the drowsiness that I have observed in those taking the waters at Sancreed, Cornwall. (Some well waters are inherently radioactive; others may simply acquire it temporarily from the granite reservoirs they are held in—presumably by radon infiltration. It is interesting that for prophecy and healing the person *came to the well or spring*: the waters had power only at their location. There is no suggestion, of course, that all holy wells have a radioactive component.) A similar drowsiness was noticed by former Dragon Project co-ordinator, John Steele, during an expedition to Bimini in the Bahamas. At one point the expedition team visited a spring in a rugged spot in North Bimini that had healing legends surrounding it and may even have been a fabled 'Fountain of Youth' referred to in early texts. After bathing in the mildly radioactive waters, a sleepiness descended on everyone (Steele, personal comment; Zink, 1979).

During 1981, writer John Sharkey and friends, engaged in one of a series of trips to Callanish on the Isle of Lewis, encountered a curious phenomenon:

> As the archaeological team were leaving [the Callanish stones] the previous year, they told us of a 'something' out on the moor and asked if we could check it out. They said lights had been seen in the sky in January [1980] and a local shepherd had reported to the police that his sheep gave a depression in the ground a wide berth. The police actually dug down straight but apparently they should have gone in at an angle of 45 degrees for if there were anything there it would be under the peat sitting on the bedrock. After an hour's search we found the spot and indeed it was the only six-foot diameter of earth on the moor that looked as if it had been dug over. Within minutes we were overcome by a series of symptoms that graduated from dizzyness to nausea to cramp in the legs to that terrible lead taste in the mouth as if every filling was about to fall out. The archaeologist had said it was 'nasty' and whatever was buried in the peat seemed to have left radioactive traces.
>
> (Sharkey, 1982)

Apart from the interesting point that the sheep reportedly sensed enough to avoid this meteorite (or whatever it was), Sharkey also told me that two other effects he and his friends noticed in the vicinity of the disturbed circle of moorland were that the awareness of any metal on one's body became very heightened, and at a certain distance from the spot a *heavy drowsiness* overtook the party.

I suspect that at particular wells or springs, *radiation languor* was one of the factors used to help induce trance-like states conducive to visionary and divinatory work. Although I do not know if the water is radioactive, it is possibly of significance that the prophetess at Delphi (see below) would drink large draughts from the Castalia spring before mounting the tripod seat to utter her vision.

In our modern, in some ways rather crude world view, we tend to think only powerful forces could possibly be used for healing effects and the creation of altered states of consciousness. But scientific research over the last few decades on the response of living organisms to magnetism, for example, has shown that creatures born and bred in the natural energy fields of the earth are able to detect and respond to very small changes in the relatively low energy levels present in those fields (see below). The same may very well apply to changes in natural radiation as well.

SPOOK ROAD

I have come to the view that certain types of radiation environments can probably help trigger a specific range of psychospiritual experiences. In Part Two I referred to the 'spook road' running alongside the Rollright circle; a stretch of this road about 360 m (400 yd) long has been found to average over three times the levels of the normal radiation background, marginally higher than the readings we obtained at Sancreed. Although it is just possible that this effect is caused by some radioactive mineral geologically deposited in a thin strip along the top of the ridge where the road happens to run, we feel it is much more likely to be due to radioactive elements in the foundation material beneath that part of the road.

However caused, the radiation levels of that strip of road are natural and were found out only by chance because of the detailed energy research going on at Rollright. It was also only because of the work

PLATE 92 Airview of the Rollright circle (King Stone at upper right-hand corner of picture) showing the radioactive length of 'spook road' immediately alongside the site.

going on at the stones that people involved in site-energy studies found themselves walking on that part of the road at various times of the day. Three people independently handed me accounts of experiences they had on that stretch of road during Dragon Project work. I alone knew that all three had been reported, and had happened precisely on the radioactive stretch of road immediately adjacent to the stone circle. (This is the first publication of this finding.) The people involved in the experiences have been known to me for years, and are totally reliable. Their reports relate to experiences that actually occurred, without doubt.

The first reported event took place on 16 February 1980. The percipient was Roy Cooper. At the time the experience took place, there had been a large group of researchers at the Rollright circle since the early hours of the morning. At 9 am, Roy left the circle and the buzz of activity there to walk out onto the road to his car, which was parked near the entrance gate:

As I left the circle through the gate I saw a car in the distance travelling towards the A34 [eastwards], and at that time approximately half a mile away...I paid little heed to it...It appeared to be travelling 35 to 40 mph, and I noticed it again as I got to my own car parked in the lay-by. I opened the boot of my car (two seconds?) and suddenly realised the other car, with two occupants, had disappeared. The disappearance struck me much more forcibly than any impression of the importance of the car initially. It certainly had not stopped in the lay-by and no way had it had time to disappear around the next bend (300 to 400 yards away) towards the A34. Either the car had disappeared or somehow I had suffered a time lapse...Usually I'm a very good judge of time, seldom wear a watch and can normally judge the time within five minutes at any time of the day and often at night as well. *The distinct and overriding impression I had was that the car had disappeared.* I've never experienced anything of this nature before...

I must stress that I did not see the car disappear—it just wasn't there any more!

The experience was so odd that I decided to keep it to myself until the end of the monitoring period.

(Cooper, 1980. Cooper's emphasis)

I was dumbfounded to receive a letter from someone else telling of another 'odd' event at the same place on 6 March. The main witness was a scientist, only slightly acquainted with the Dragon Project, who has asked for anonymity. He had dropped by to visit one of the monitors on an Operation Merlin session at the Rollright circle. Afterwards, the witness returned to his van parked in the smaller of the two lay-bys near the circle. It was 1.45 pm. Grabbing a bite of a sandwich, he was talking to another colleague while sitting in the van when he suddenly 'saw the back of a dog pass the [passenger] window from left to right. It was dark grey and short-haired, and I didn't see its head'. The creature did not emerge in front of the van, so the two men opened the door of the vehicle and looked out, 'but there was nothing to be seen' (personal communication, 11 March 1980).

'On reflection,' the witness added in his letter, 'there seems no reason for me to call the object a dog, but I was convinced *immediately* (and not on reflection because the time was far too short for that) that it was.' I personally questioned the man, and apart from the inexplicable disappearance of the animal, it was also clear that in order for its back to have been seen above the bottom of the van window the 'dog' must have stood about 1.2 m (4 ft) tall at the shoulder!

The third case that was reported to me as occurring along this specific length of road happened on 25 October 1981. The percipient was Caroline Wise. By now the radioactive nature of the patch of road had become apparent to core members of the Dragon Project, though its precise extent and its comparison to other radiation levels was at that time unknown. At the time of the incident, Wise was in her late twenties, and she had (and continues to have) a personal and professional interest in psi research. Allowing for these factors, however, I am in no doubt at all regarding the actuality of the events the witness describes. She makes no claims as to personal psychic ability.

·She was observing the work of two dowsers from the British Society of Dowsers at work on the King's Men site on behalf of the Dragon Project. They had been there for some hours, and it was now early afternoon. Wise absent-mindedly strolled along the road where it comes closest to the circle:

> I glanced down at the road surface and watched it form into a pattern of concentric circles about seven inches in diameter. Simultaneously, I felt like I was vibrating, especially inside my head. It was like a 'buzzing', and it seemed I was enveloped in a highly charged atmosphere...I was looking at the circles, and suddenly became aware that the event was not normal! The road instantly returned to how it looked before. I looked up, and saw an old-fashioned gypsy caravan; it was green wood and the horsedrawn type. I saw it from behind. It was going away from us but hadn't passed us. Again, I didn't think it was odd. I glanced away, and when I looked back, the caravan had vanished. This whole incident lasted only a few seconds and the whole feeling during the event was lazy, contented.

(Personal communication, 1987)

Old style gypsy caravans would certainly have travelled along the old ridgeway in bygone times.

It might also be significant that the strange 'cloud' in an infra-red photograph referred to in Part Two was apparently hovering over this stretch of road.

BOLEIGH

Another spot with similar levels of natural radiation is Boleigh fogou (Part Two), and it has already been mentioned that people have claimed psychic episodes there. One report (passed on to me by the kind intervention of Cheryl Straffon, editress of *Meyn Mamvro*), involves a woman (who seeks anonymity) who spent time alone in the fogou at night:

> As I stood there in the dark, I began to feel strangely without identity or time: I was a woman in any age...Suddenly it was no longer dark but I appeared to be standing in daylight a little way away from a church and watching a wedding party coming out of the church. The bride, groom and guests were there although I could not see faces clearly. It was a bit like watching a video in the clarity of the picture. Then I remember being distracted and feeling cold and the vision disappeared and went out. This was a bizarre experience...you could say that I must have dozed off and dreamed it, but for me the clarity and lucidity of the images made it different from a dream. In any case I was vertical the whole time and I remember thinking to myself 'Well, how odd this is!'

Another important experience associated with Boleigh fogou was, of course, Jo May's observation of small-scale light phenomena dancing over the internal surfaces of the roofing stones. This was almost identical to the Barnatt and Larkman observations inside Chûn Quoit. This type of light phenomenon seems to be another characteristic of enclosed environments with high natural radiation. But it is only by the greatest good fortune that we now have a record of its existence—not too many people sit at night inside Neolithic dolmens or Iron Age fogous!

It is just possible, I suppose, that the lights are created as phosphenes in the observer's retina—maybe by the radiation in the atmosphere—but I have discussed the observations with the people concerned, and all have been adamant that the lights were external, objective phenomena, occurring on or just above the surface of the stone. They are not *psi* (psychic) events. My guess would be that they are some result of ionization in the air inside these granitic structures, perceptible only in near total darkness with finely adjusted night vision. These rock lights would have provided another means whereby the ancient megalith builders could have become aware of radiation in stone. And there is no way these people would have been unaware of these 'fairy lights' that would naturally have made a big impression, and rightly so. If the larger, outdoors earth lights were brought into their spiritual belief systems, these smaller, luminescent, rock phenomena must likewise have been incorporated. And they would have been *used*: primary peoples everywhere used whatever was in their natural surroundings to further their psychospiritual pursuits, which were always of paramount importance. This factor is given insufficient weight by orthodox researchers.

NATURAL RADIOACTIVITY AND ALTERED STATES

This brings us back to the *psi* effects. It seems to me that a characteristic of radiation-*psi* is a sense of a time-slip—the percipient is momentarily lifted out of his or her space-time and a view of the past (or possibly future) flashes into awareness. If such effects were first noted near granite outcrops and other sources of localized radioactivity, the stone would in many societies have come to be used in structures designed to augment practices aimed at producing mind-change.

We have hints of this in ancient Egypt. Let us take a look at the King's Chamber in the Great Pyramid at Giza. Too much has been written about the mysteries of the Great Pyramid to attempt even a synopsis here. What can be simply stated about it is that it certainly encodes fundamental measurements and ratios relating to the dimensions of the Earth, though some interpretations of what is supposed to be contained in the Great Pyramid's structure do enter the realm of 'pyramidiocy', to use the term coined by the late Glyn Daniel.

Access to the King's Chamber, positioned high up within the

PLATE 93 The Great Pyramid, Giza, from the south-east.

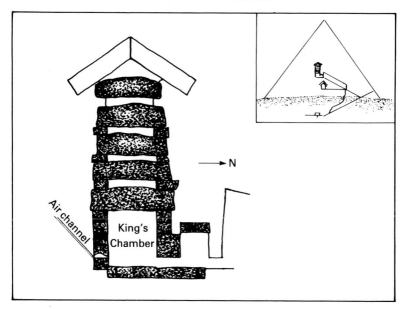

FIG. 27 Elevation of the King's Chamber, showing tiered slabs above the chamber roof. Granite is depicted in heavy texture. Inset: the general positions of King's Chamber and other chambers and passages within the Great Pyramid.

Pyramid, is initially by means of a low passageway that has an almost machine-like finish to it. This then opens out into a high passage called the Grand Gallery that inclines steeply for 48 m (157 ft) to the King's Chamber. This passage is of breathtaking exactitude, with polished stone surfaces. As John Anthony West correctly observes (1985): 'It is difficult to avoid the impression that you are in the inside of an enormous instrument of some sort'. There can be no doubt about the geodetic, metrological, and engineering significance of the Great Pyramid. It is awesome and a challenge to the curiously narrow view modern scholarship tries to foist upon the past. But my concern here is to look at just one aspect of this Old Kingdom edifice.

The Pyramid as a whole is built from limestone. But the King's Chamber is constructed from Aswan granite, quarried 965 km (600 miles) away to the south. Granite was spirit stone to the ancient Egyptians, and inside the King's Chamber one does not doubt it. Its walls are made of exactly 100 granite blocks fitted together with utter precision. The floor is granite. The roof is formed by nine granite slabs, some weighing over 50 tonnes. Out of sight above that ceiling is a series of rough granite blocks ascending one above another, with spaces between them.

PLATE 94 The damaged sarcophagus in the King's Chamber. Granite within granite . . .

The walls of the King's Chamber (and the entrance passages) are devoid of any inscriptions. At the west end of the chamber is a slightly damaged granite sarcophagus without a lid. It is too big to have been brought through the entrance passage. It is empty. Plain. To the modern archaeologist it has been robbed; to the esotericist it was used for initiatory practice and never had a mummy or grave goods within it. And what tomb robber would bother to struggle away with the lid of the sarcophagus?

To stand alone within the chamber is an awesome, profoundly eerie experience. It is a dark and sombre place. I took radiation measurements of the granite walls. The readings were of course much higher than the desert background. Surprisingly, the readings for the interior of the sarcophagus, granite within granite, were the same as for the walls' surfaces. The biggest surprise was that the *air count* in the middle of the chamber was substantially higher than the granite surfaces themselves—36 per cent higher on the day I monitored it. This was presumably due to radon being pumped out by the granite on every side and simply accumulating within the chamber. The readings were similar to those obtained in some of the Cornish stone chambers.

I have no doubt in my own mind that this radiation-spiced air was intended to be breathed. The chamber has two air ducts leading to it—the only inference can be that the chamber was meant to be used by the living. And if that was the case, then the place must have been for psychospiritual activities. The radon atmosphere would have been one element used to help induce certain mental states. In his 1930s book, *A*

PLATE 95 *Right*: The author in the gloomy, radon-permeated King's Chamber.

Search in Secret Egypt, Paul Brunton described an out-of-the-body he had when he spent the night alone in the chamber, for example.

Fig. 28 shows (upper line) the comparative levels of radiation obtained by the same instrument at a number of the sites discussed in this book, including the King's Chamber. The lower line shows the background environmental readings for the same places. The instrument's manufacturers say that normal, average background-readings with the machine will be about 12 cpm; in the figure the total average of background radiation to the sacred sites is in fact 12.4 cpm. The sites themselves average 26.6 cpm. We can see from the figure that sites individually range between two and three times higher than their local environments. It would seem that radiation around this level can trigger *psi*-episodes in some people, and can also cause unusual objective luminescent effects in enclosed, bare-granite chambers. If the sceptic baulks at the former suggestion due to modern cultural conditioning, the second can be tested.

Some of the granite cottages in Cornwall probably have similar levels of radiation to certain of the megalithic enclosures. (I measured one house, and found it to have slightly lower counts than any of the sites indicated in Fig. 28.) In a house situation, with plastering, decoration, lighting, and so on, it is most unlikely any light phenomena would be evident, and it is probable that the inhabitants of a house would rarely be in the right mental frame to encourage *psi* phenomena. Nevertheless, it would probably be a worthwhile psychic-research project by some

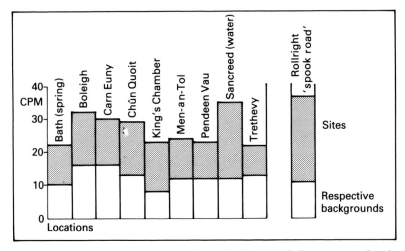

FIG. 28 Histogram showing actual comparisons of radiation levels (in counts per minute) at certain sites, and at the segment of Rollright 'spook road' where monitoring with the same instrument has taken place, along with their respective background readings. See text for further discussion.

suitable organization to carry out a survey of granite-built houses in Cornwall with high radon levels to see how the incidence of reported spontaneous *psi* phenomena in them compares with a set of low-radon dwellings. In *Earth Lights Revelation*, I give a full account of an English-woman who lives on top of a granite hill in South America. Not only is there sporadic earth light phenomena outside the place, the woman reports curious time shifts and the momentary appearance and dis-appearance of objects or entities inside her home. This type of experi-ence seems characteristic of radiation-*psi*.

The world's greatest megalithic complex is found in granitic Brit-tany, and the French writer Marc Dem notes that France is the fourth most important producer of uranium in the West. The areas of France with the highest megalithic density correspond with uranium-rich zones. In Britain, where there is little uranium, megalithic areas correspond with 'extensive but weak uranium deposits' and areas of 'many anomalies' (Dem, 1977). Swiss researcher Blanche Mertz has remarked that some of the great Tibetan monastries are in an area of 'higher than normal radioactivity', and she has measured high counts at numerous temples, such as that of Lakham Soma at Alchi. 'The power points of monasteries are situated on the granite in this zone, and the builders certainly chose their sites in relation to the play of natural forces,' Mertz writes (1987). Mount Harney in South Dakota figures prominently in the Great Vision of Black Elk of the Oglala Sioux (Neihardt, 1972)—we now know the peak is a uranium mountain. As John Steele has pointed out, the 'land rights' controversies in America and Australia arise because uranium deposits have been found in areas that the indigenous peoples, the Indians and Aborigines respectively, think of as sacred. One Indian Elder remarked that only the white man would think of taking uranium out of the ground—in the earth it was part of the natural order, but removed it became deadly in itself and the land it was taken from became de-natured.

In south-west USA, fogou-like structures are also to be found—the *kivas* of the Pueblo Indians. These subterranean and semi-underground ritual and ceremonial enclosures are found in an area of some of the greatest uranium deposits in North America. I have noted that general background radiation readings in New Mexico, for example, match exactly the high backgrounds found in Cornwall.

GEOPSYCHEDELIA

Radiation-*psi* would be only one factor in achieving altered states. Fasting, initiatory ordeal, heat, chanting, hypnosis, rhythm, dancing, and intoxicants were all used in various combinations and perhaps for slightly different ends. Inside the Kuaua *kiva* near Santa Fe, were some of the finest examples of pre-Columbian painting to have been found in the USA: a series of wall paintings dating back to the fourteenth century. One of these murals showed an almost lifesize Medicine Man holding Jimson Weed. This plant is a powerful hallucinogen, and tells us unequivocally of an aspect of *kiva* usage.

Use of hallucinogenic (psychoactive; psychedelic) substances has occurred throughout human history. Fifty thousand years ago, a man was buried in a cave in northern Iraq along with a range of flowers (Leroy-Gourham, 1975) which were psychoactive (Mankowicz, undated). Evidence of this sort is said to go back 100,000 years. Highly scholarly research has indicated that hallucinogens may have been the foundation of later world religions, and R. Gordon Wasson proposed that the psychoactive mushroom, *Amanita muscaria*, may have been the legendary *soma*. He also put forward the theory that the wine used at the Mysteries of Eleusis in ancient Greece may have been made from ergot-tainted grain (ergot gives LSD-like effects). Plato, Socrates, and Pythagoras took part in these mysteries. It is certainly the case that hallucinogens were (and are) the cornerstone of shamanic practices around the world. It is in the use of such substances that we can clearly see the opportunism of primary cultures with regard to their access of altered states. An Indian in Mexico, for instance, might use the peyote

PLATE 96   The interior of the heavily-restored Kuaua *kiva*, New Mexico. One of the figures depicted in the ancient mural paintings found in this *kiva* holds Jimson Weed, a hallucinogenic plant.

cactus for attaining altered states of consciousness. But this was not available in, say, Britain, so the prehistoric British shaman would use something else that was available in the local environment—probably the psilocybin mushroom. Different substances were used around the world depending on availability. The purposes were the same and the effects of the hallucinogens powerfully influenced the outlook of the cultures or tribal groupings in which they were used. Different hallucinogens would have different characteristics, however, and these would colour the societies involved (McKenna, 1988).

Our culture abhors mind-altering substances, and makes little social or legal discrimination between psychedelic agents and narcotics. Part of the cultural fear of psychedelic ('mind-manifesting') substances stems from the explosive social use of LSD in the 1960s, and its connotations of rebelling youth and access to states of mind outside the jurisdiction of the prevailing cultural world view. It is difficult for us, therefore, to realize that such substances were held in reverence and awe by early peoples. Indeed, they were viewed as sacramental—and still are in some surviving tribal groups. As the clinical psychologist Richard Yensen (1988) has written:

Psychedelic compounds are not new and they are *not associated with countercultural forces in the rituals of traditional cultures*. In fact, traditional societies use them as a powerful tool for renewing and transmitting the basic belief systems of their cultures.

The importance given to the magico-religious role of, say, the Cornish fogous can be discerned by the archaeological evidence at Carn Euny (Part Two) alone: the beehive hut and fogou were the first major, permanent structures to be built at the site. We can make an educated guess at how these places were used. We can envisage the use of ceremonial dancing, chanting, and drum-beating in the fogou (as in the Kiva Dance of the Pueblo Indians), against a social background of myths and belief systems, as preparatory activities to the taking of the sacred mushroom or other hallucinogens. The geophysical properties (as we would call them) of the fogou would act on the participants' levels of consciousness, which would be rendered mobile and fluid by ritual and the psychoactive substances, so the effect of the radiation would be infinitely enhanced. The existence of the rock lights would be used, and we may tentatively suspect a psychic interaction between participants and the lightforms within the otherwise dark radioactive interior of the fogou.

The energy of the fogou was thus doubtlessly just one of the tools used by those Celtic peoples in their requirement for altered states of consciousness. As Eliade has stated (1964), shamanism is primarily a collection of pragmatic techniques for attaining ecstasy.

Different rituals, myths, and beliefs were probably associated with the use of the much earlier dolmen structures, but the ends would be the same. Such experiences would be associated with the passage of the spirit from the body and thus connotations with death would be obvious. This may be the reason we occasionally find evidence of the ritual use of human and animal bones at such places—such 'bone displays' are known to relate to initiatory practice in other cultures. But the light phenomena inside the dolmen (or fogou or other enclosure) were for the use of the living—and may even have been perceived as the spirits of the ancestors, of the Dead.

Psychedelics are primarily used today either in medical, laboratory settings or carelessly 'for kicks'. For their sacramental, shamanic dimension in some societies we must picture their carefully projected use in environments that were both psychologically *and geophysically* enhancing. Such conditions may have allowed a unique type of contact with the forces of nature, with the presence of the planet, quite unknown to the modern mind. We could term this archaic and largely lost practice of mind-change *geopsychedelia*, the development of an earth-mind, a psychospiritual kinship with place beyond modern understanding.

MAGNETIC SENSITIVITY

Another aspect of the geophysical properties of sacred sites would have been magnetism. The guide in Part Two identified some sites that either possess natural magnetic anomalies themselves, or have had them imported and incorporated in the form of individual stones.

The megalith builders could have identified the presence of the unusual magnetism by use of an 'instrument' that could have been applied at any time in human prehistory—a piece of magnetite on a thread; a lodestone. The behaviour of such a 'magic stone' near certain outcrops would identify a magnetic anomaly—the presence of spirit. But such a method may not have been necessary. While contemporary research has little to say about human direct-sensing of radiation, it more readily accepts the reality of magnetic sensitivity.

It is now known, after a long period of scientific disbelief, that a whole variety of living systems can be sensitive to low levels of magnetism. Science has only relatively recently become aware that organisms can respond to such weak stimuli as changes in geomagnetism, yet, when one thinks about it, it is only to be expected that creatures brought up within the energy fields of the earth should have their biological sensitivities attuned to those levels.

Researchers have found that bacteria can respond to the North Pole or to a magnet moved around them, and that snails and worms can detect incredibly weak magnetic fields. Soviet scientists have found that geomagnetic-field variations can affect the growth of mushrooms and the development of the nervous system in an embryo. Such plants as the herbs mugwort or succory are responsive to magnetic influence, their leaves turn themselves to the north like the needle of a compass. It is now known that pigeons can navigate by the use of their sensitivity to the geomagnetic field in addition to other direction-finding aids, such as the position of the sun, while whales and dolphins seem able to cruise along 'magnetic stripes' laid out on the ocean floors due to tectonic action. Other creatures scientifically tested and found to possess magnetic sensitivity include algae, crabs, salmon, honey bees, salamanders, robins, mice. And so on. The list of lifeforms sensitive to subtle levels of magnetism is now very long. It has been shown in experiments with some animals that they can detect magnetic levels below a thousandth of a gauss (remember the earth's field strength is about half a gauss!). Work at the University of Hawaii and the

California Institute of Technology has suggested that the sensitivity to magnetic change of the yellowfin tuna could be in the order of one nanotesla—less than one twenty-thousandth of the earth's field (Williamson, 1987).

If other organisms can detect magnetism, what about human beings? Dr Michael Shallis has found that profoundly electrically sensitive people tend to suffer from allergies, which may have an electrical basis. One of Shallis' subjects was not only phenomenally responsive to electrical fields, but also to magnetism:

> When he is ill from his allergies he finds the telephone helps him to recover: he says the magnet in the earpiece seems to stabilise his immune system. More dramatic is his sensitivity to the Earth's magnetic field: When his allergy reactions debilitate him, he becomes acutely aware of direction. If he faces north he feels better and rather euphoric. Facing or moving south makes his symptoms worse and can even provoke unconsciousness. East–west directions seem neutral to him. As he lives north of the allergy clinic, travelling southwards to it is a hazardous journey for him and he can pass out *en route*. There have been times when he has had to be taken to the clinic by a circuitous route, tacking eastwards and westwards rather like a yacht against the wind, in order to minimise the southward passage of his movement.
>
> (Shallis, 1988)

During many years of controlled tests with dowsers in Virginia, USA, Harvalik (above) was able to provide experimental evidence that human beings could achieve incredible sensitivity to magnetism. Harvalik himself could not help remarking that 'one is utterly amazed by the sensitivity of the human body to such [magnetic] anomalies. Magnetometric measurements indicate that a dowser reacts to magnetic gradient changes as weak as one millimicrogauss, or, expressed another way, 10^{-9}, or 0.00000001 gauss' (Bird, 1979). His work with the late Wilhelm de Boer, the German master dowser, indicated that the man could be sensitive to a phenomenal 10^{-13} gauss. Harvalik found that most beginners could be trained into surprising levels of magnetic sensitivity. Abilities seemed to be helped by the ingestion of water prior to tests. Physicist Yves Rocard, a professor at the Ecole Normale in Paris, has similarly been able to show that human beings can detect magnetic changes down to 10^{-8} gauss.

In pigeons and numerous other magnetically sensitive creatures— even in some of the bacteria—small grains of magnetite have been found. It is as if these organisms are carrying their own biological compass—or lodestone, at any rate. Does it exist in humans? Dr Robin Baker of the Department of Zoology at Manchester University, thinks it probably does. By the early 1980s Baker and his team had detected a thin embedded layer of high-iron content in the bones forming the walls of the sinuses—the deep-seated sphenoid-ethmoid sinus complex that is in close proximity to parts of the brain.

Even with this magnetic centre, human beings would need to train themselves to use it readily. Testing of direction-finding in humans is still going on at the time of writing, but the results of earlier experiments of this sort do seem to provide some evidence of an inherent direction-finding ability in humans.

Baker's work has been done on modern skulls: one wonders if the sinus iron-deposits were greater in people of the third and second millennia BC (when, incidentally, the earth's field may have been stronger) due to different diet and other factors.

MAGNETISM IN THE ANCIENT WORLD

We have seen in the guide that there are magnetic stones at some stone circles, and there are hundreds of sites yet to check. Magnetic associations with megaliths and other ancient sites have been sporadically noted in other parts of the world, but no one has yet begun to look seriously at this aspect of prehistoric sites, so there are no lists in existence as yet. All that can be done here is to give a few examples.

Mark Lynch, working as research assistant to Dr Lawrence H. Robbins of Michigan State University, has noted magnetic anomalies at the Namoratunga II site near Lake Turkana in Kenya. There are several stone circles at the site and two rows of unworked stone pillars, one running east–west, the other north–south. These rows are enclosed by a 15-m (50-ft) diameter circle comprised of small boulders.

PLATE 97 Magnetic monitoring for the Dragon Project on the Kermario stone-row complex, Carnac, Brittany.

Lynch found several of the pillars to be magnetic, sending his compass spinning. The layout of the rows to the cardinal points suggests a deliberate knowledge of this by the builders.

At the greatest megalithic complex of them all, around Carnac-Ville in Brittany, Belgian researcher Pierre Méreaux has found an interesting magnetic pattern. The most famous of the Carnac area's thousands of megaliths are the great multiple rows of standing stones forming several groups of alignments. Méreaux took 240 magnetic readings with a sensitive instrument:

> The whole area included between the alignments, from the west of Erdeven to the northeast of Carnac, shows a very stable magnetic field, with slight negative or positive variations in the order of 10 gammas. The alignments proper form a precise frontier to this zone, and the field begins to be disturbed in the middle of the field of menhirs, where the variations already reach 200 to 250 gammas. At Kermario, Kerlescan and at Le Menec, to the south of the alignments, outside the zone studied, the disturbances vary between −400 and +1100 gammas. The only exception concerns the rows of standing stones of Kerkerho at Erdeven, where the stable magnetic field passes slightly outside of the rows of menhirs, next to the two great stones standing to the north of the alignment.
>
> Even while staying within the cautious limits of a certain scientific rigour, this would seem to demonstrate that the fields of menhirs of this area were not planted there by chance and that their presence would be in direct relation to terrestrial magnetism... This may be summarised by a double question: 'Were the menhirs raised there because of the curious characteristics of the place, or does the place have curious characteristics because of the presence of the menhirs?'
>
> (Méreaux et al., 1981)

Also in France, Blanche Mertz has found three magnetic anomalies at the 'Stones of Acq' near the village of Ecoivres, in the Pas-de-Calais in the north of the country. One stone is over 2.5 m (8 ft) tall and its companion rises to slightly more than 3.10 m (10 ft). They form a north-west–south-east alignment, with one magnetic-anomaly spot lying between them, one immediately to their north, and the third just to their west.

On the pampa near Nasca, Peru, are the famous 'Nasca lines': hundreds of dead straight lines covering the desert surface. No one knows who marked them on the desert pavement nor what their purpose could possibly be. They were probably produced during the first millennium AD, though some may be older. Sprinkled amongst the lines are giant drawings of creatures, spirals, and abstract designs. Maria Reiche, a German mathematician now in her nineties, has dedicated half her life to the study of the lines. She is not a woman given to thoughtless frivolity, so her brief comments on unusual phenomena amidst the lines, recorded in Tony Morrison's *The Mystery of the Nasca Lines* (1987), carry particular weight. 'There is one place on the pampa which is very strange,' Reiche stated:

> I found it when I was measuring...No, perhaps I'd better not say where it is, but anyway that doesn't matter too much—it's a place where the compass doesn't work. The needle stops at any point on the dial and you lose yourself very easily...someone once said it could be caused by a large piece of buried metal.

Maria Reiche has also noted moving lights on the desert.

As far as magnetic stones at sites are concerned, I suspect they were employed for both healing work and as another geophysical means of augmenting altered states of consciousness.

Modern medicine uses pulsed low-frequency magnetic fields to treat bone fractures (and folklore tells us that bone disorders were one of the chief ailments brought to the stones for treatment), and some forms of alternative medicine today use the application of magnets to treat certain disorders. In Japan, for instance, they are thought to help arthritis and rheumatism, and the Russians use water exposed to magnetism to ease painful urination. There are claims of magnetic fields inhibiting the spread of tumours. Folklore from the earliest times tells of the healing properties of magnets and the lodestone. There are references in early Vedic scripts to the use of the magnet for stopping bleeding; it is said that Egyptian noblewomen would wear a magnet, and there are references to the therapeutic use of magnets from the ancient Greeks through to the Middle Ages.

Elizabeth Pepper and John Wilcock write (1977):

> Occultists have long associated the magnet with the magic (magnetic) wand of Hermes (Mercury)...Some say Asclepius was the son of Hermes and he, too, had a magic rod, the famous wand 'through the possession of which a man becomes the master of healing.'
>
> Homer, Pythagoras, Epicurus, Aristotle—all were familiar with the magnet, and the Renaissance magus Agrippa also alluded to it...
>
> Claudian's *Riddles of the Magnet* refers to...the magnetic image of Venus held suspended in the air at one of the temples, an iron one of Mars at another. 'The war-like Mars loves the magnet,' is, in the Orphic poetry, our first encounter with the word...
>
> In his *History of Magic*, Joseph Ennemoser...says that priests traditionally guarded their knowledge about magnetism from the uninitiated...There are frequent references in ancient Egyptian writings, he explains, to temple images suspended by what must clearly be magnetic force...

Magnetism...constitutes an art of healing, not through a substance but by a power, a power borrowed 'from the stars and nowhere else,' says Paracelsus, the sixteenth-century alchemist.

Paracelsus attributed many of his healing powers to magnetism, offering precise instructions on laying the magnet in the center from which the sickness proceeds. 'It is not a matter of indifference to which of these poles a man applies.' People had something magnetic in them, he maintained, without which they could not exist and through which they were linked to the sun and the stars.

MAGNETIC MIND-GATES

It is known that the temporal-lobe area of the brain is sensitive to electromagnetism, and parts of the temporal lobe, such as the hippocampus, are related to dreaming and to memory. Magnetic fields can stimulate these parts of the brain, and Professor Michael Persinger of Laurentian University has made considerable study of this (see the author's *Earth Lights Revelation* for a longer discussion of his work). Stimulation of these brain regions seems able to produce in the subject sensations of floating, even out-of-the-body sensations, the production of vivid hallucinatory images into waking consciousness, and mystical and visionary states. Persinger and colleagues have produced some exciting statistical evidence that suggests that there is a link between some forms of *psi* activity in humans and the activity of the geomagnetic field (see, for example, Persinger and Schaut, 1988).

Robert O. Becker notes (1985) that the anthropologist and pharmacologist Francis Ivanhoe has suggested that 'the hippocampus...acts as a transducer of electromagnetic energy. A part of the hippocampus called Ammon's horn, an arch with one-way nerve traffic directed by a strong current flow, may read out variations in the [Earth's] field strength' feeding them to other parts of the brain. Becker adds (*ibid.*): 'The idea gains further support from the fact that neural activity in the hippocampus increases with electrical stimulation and reaches a maximum at 10 to 15 cycles per second, or slightly above the dominant micropulsation of today's field'.

Another factor that may be significant is that with the recent advent of the super-sensitive SQUID magnetometer it has been discovered that the human head produces a weak magnetic field of its own. Perhaps this field can act as a kind of interface between the brain and variable magnetic fields in the environment.

We can only speculate, of course, but it does seem at least a possibility that St Brynach, probably sensitized by fasting and meditative prayer, was assisted in his discourse with the angels by sitting in the fossilized reversed-geomagnetic fields on top of Carn Ingli (Part Two).

In the case of the smaller anomalies offered by the 'magnetic stones' in stone circles, I imagine that close contact would be essential (as it would, presumably, for the high-radiation stones noted at some circles), whether for healing or mind-change purposes. One can perhaps envisage the prehistoric shaman, after dancing and chanting, under the influence of magic mushrooms or some toxic herbal infusion, spreading himself or herself against the magic stone for entry to the spirit world.

One of these anomaly stones occurs at Gors Fawr in Wales, as noted in the guide. It has a curious shape that actually encourages one to *sit* on it. The sitter's head leans back against exactly that part of the stone that most disturbs the compass: the cerebral cortex is in close proximity to the natural magnetic effect. The stone is also involved in a midsummer-sunrise alignment. Would the effect be somehow enhanced then? Or does that clue tell us when the ritual was carried out at the magnetic 'spirit' stone? Alas, we have much yet to learn in our fledgling study of geopsychedelics.

A similar kind of 'seat' was also noted at the magnetic serpentine outcrop on Mount Tamalpais (see Plate 97 above). Sitting there, one's spine is kept comfortably but firmly erect. It may be that close contact with these special forms of natural magnetism have different effects to artificial magnets.

8   SOUND AND LIGHT

At this stage, there can be little more than speculation about natural radiation and magnetism, the two most commonly encountered measurable forces at sites so far studied, but the markers have certainly been put down for further research of all kinds—'fringe' and orthodox. Both types need doing. There is even less that can be said at this time about most of the other possible energy effects noted in this book. It is appropriate, however, to record some final thoughts regarding the two other main energy anomalies that research has suggested might be associated with ancient sacred places—ultrasound and geological light phenomena.

DAWN SONG

Is ultrasound a real phenomenon at Rollright and other sites, some other signal masquerading as ultrasound, or a spurious effect? Until more, intensive dawn work is done, with an enhanced range of equipment, we simple cannot be sure. But it does remain a possibility that this is a real phenomenon. I am inclined to this view because apart from the coincidence that at least three different kinds of ultrasound detector—and only ultrasound detectors—have picked up the curious signals reported in Part Two, there is the testimony of audible sound being heard at stones from time to time, as we have also noted. It could be that the audible sound is related to an ultrasonic effect, with some factor temporarily lowering the frequency, thus bringing the pressure wave down into the range of human hearing. Something like this may have happened at the Colossi of Memnon, near the Valley of the Kings in Egypt.

These two 18-m (60-ft) tall statues represent Amenhotep III, and are all that remains of the King's mortuary temple. Each figure of the king is flanked by smaller figures of the queen mother and his wife. In 27 BC an earthquake damaged the northern colossus, after which it emitted a sound at sunrise. Descriptions of this sound vary: it was a soft, bell-like sound according to some contemporary commentators, a musical note

PLATE 98 The Colossi of Memnon, Egypt. The statue on the right was the one that used to issue a musical note at dawn.

to others, while yet others claimed it was more like a trumpet blast or even a sound like a cord snapping. The phenomenon was widely referred to by the writers of antiquity, and the site became an attraction for Greek tourists of the day. The statue was used as an oracle. But in the early third century AD, Septimius Severus had the statue repaired in the somewhat clumsy fashion still visible today. This change to the structure stopped the occurrence of the dawn sounds. The Colossus fell silent.

The widespread accounts of the dawn sound, the proven use of the Colossus as an oracle, and the fact that the repairs were universally claimed to have stopped the effect, all suggest the phenomenon actually occurred. Modern commentators have suggested the sound could have been caused by wind blowing through cracks in the sculpture, or the rising sun's rays causing expansion in the cracks. But in view of the apparent ultrasound signals received from the British megaliths, also at dawn, we might also suggest that the statue emitted ultrasound until it was damaged in the earthquake, after which the deformation to its structure lowered the frequency of the ultrasound into the audible range. It is also of interest to note that the Colossi, which face the rising sun, are made from a sandstone that is not local to the area—it must have been brought from at least 160 km (100 miles) away—and that was most unsuitable for such huge, outdoor sculpture because it is difficult to work and subject to rapid erosion, as can be seen from the state of the figures today. It is widely believed by 'alternative' Egypto-logists that the Egyptian masons incorporated sonic factors into their structures. The stones of the Rollright circle are also sandstone.

If ultrasound does occur at the megaliths, what would its uses have been? We can only project from what we currently know. Ultrasound can be used for healing, and is now so employed in modern medicine. And seeds bathed in ultrasound are said to germinate more rapidly, so there could have been a fecundity aspect to the phenomenon.

How is the ultrasound produced, if it is present at all? That remains a mystery. Don Robins has suggested that microwave energy from the rising sun might energize electrons held in energy traps inside a stone's atomic lattice. Microwave energy has been shown experimentally to be able to transduce through the lattice structure to emerge as a pressure wave. The frequencies of the energies involved would mean the pressure wave would manifest as ultrasound (Robins, 1985). It is a neat theory, but there are many objections to it, and the preferred occurrence of the signal at dawn rather than sunset is not explained, nor is its absence altogether on most sunrises. The whole ultrasound matter remains unsure and enigmatic.

EARTH LIGHTS TRADITIONS

Then there is the question of the earth light phenomena at megalithic sites in Britain. It has been argued by a small number of scientists and other researchers, including myself, that these lights occur by prefer-ence in areas of faulting and associated geological disturbance. Paul McCartney (Part One) has shown that stone circles, at least, are also situated near faulting. But the circles are permanent and the cyclic or sporadic lights are transient, so it is difficult to provide hard evidence of an association between lights and sites. Nevertheless, as the guide in Part Two clearly indicates, the coincidences are beginning to accumu-late.

The lights would be seen, their habits and habitat noted, and sites erected in the vicinity of regular appearances. Perhaps the lights were seen as expressions of a deity or as spirits. Perhaps they were used in ritual or magical practice in some way; there may have been human interaction with them.

None of this is as speculative as it may sound. Traditional societies known to us were definitely aware of these lights and incorporated them into their world view. The Yakima Indians in Washington State, USA, used them for divinatory purposes, and the Snohomish Indians of the same general area of north-west USA (where Kenneth Arnold saw the first 'flying saucers' in 1947) see such lights as 'doorways' into the Otherworld. Mircea Eliade (1964) refers to an Iglulik Eskimo woman who became a shamaness 'as the result of a fireball entering her body'. The Mexican Tzeltal distinguish between red, green, and yellow balls of fire. The Penobscot Indians of North America see lightballs as *eskuda'hit* ('fire creatures') or *medeoli'nuwak*, flying shamans magically transformed into lightballs. Californian Indian tribes see the lights as 'spirit eaters'—it is dangerous to get near them. This is echoed by the belief of the indigenous people of the Himalayan foothills in north-west India that such lights are 'little men' carrying lanterns who will cause illness or death if encountered too closely. To Malaysian natives, earth lights are the ghostly heads of women who died in childbirth. Australian aborigines see their 'min min lights' as spirits of the ancestors or the machinations of shamans. Chinese Buddhists used to see the lights as manifestations of the Dharma, and even built temples to observe them (Blofeld, 1972). The Japanese saw such lights as flying spirits, as do the Hawaiian islanders, who call them *Akualele*. To the African Ewe people they are produced by the magic of ju-ju men. Lights in the sky over Lapland are shamans in battle (sometimes an interpretation given to the Northern Lights as well)—'Fire Lapps'. To earlier Europeans, the lights were spirits of the Dead, hovered over buried treasure, or indicated mineral deposits.

Such examples are legion. It is only our lonely, solitary culture that chooses not to see the lights. Indeed, it is its energetically maintained belief structure—no more valid than those listed above—that the lights do not exist. The psychological basis of our world view cannot allow them to.

Referring to shamans, the German ethnopsychologist, Holger Kalweit, notes (1988): 'Inner luminosity is often preceded by a visible physical phenomenon of light, such as a ball of fire, lightning, pillars of fire, a figure of light, or simply a light beam'. Similarly, modern 'UFO' close-encounter witnesses also frequently report a new-found psychic, healing, or spiritual ability after their experience. This is probably because these lights are comprised of a currently unknown form of energy, which seems to possess some remarkable and distinctly weird qualities, producing profound alterations in consciousness when in close proximity to a person. (All these matters are dealt with at greater length in my *Earth Lights Revelation*.)

SITES AND FAULTS

The siting of the circles and some other sites on or close to faulting is a fact—but can it have been a deliberate act by the megalith builders? Many sceptics think that it is merely a fortuitous coincidence, and read no significance into it. Four thousand years later, it is obviously not now possible to prove intent on the part of the stone-circle architects, but we can look elsewhere for corroborative evidence.

As a first example, let us take the ruins of the Anasazi, the mysterious lost people, the 'Old Ones', of the American south-west, who were active during the first millennium AD. One of their major sites is at Wupatki, north of Flagstaff in Arizona. Journalist Susan Benner describes a visit there (1988) and makes a relevant observation:

> Behind the Wupatki visitor center is a pueblo known as Wupatki, the largest and most elaborate in the park...the pueblo was built by the Singua people, probably under the tutelage of the Kayenta. It may have had as many as 100 rooms, as well as a circular ceremonial structure that resembles the kivas of the Anasazi and Pueblo tribes...the stone-work...has the Anasazi grace of harmony with its surroundings...
>
> One of the unexplained clues to the relationship of these people to the earth is a hole in the ground, one of several openings to a seven billion cubic foot system of underground faults. Called a blow hole, the opening typically takes in cold heavy air at night and expels air during the day when the air outside is warmer and lighter...The significance of blow holes and earth cracks to the builders of the pueblos is not known...but many of the pueblos in this area are built near them.

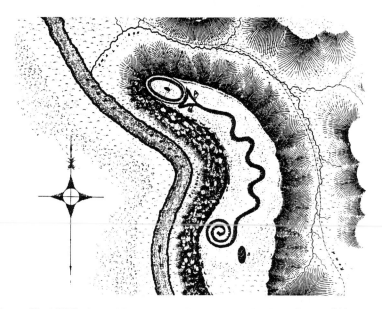

FIG. 29 The 1846 Squier and Davis survey of Serpent Mound, Adams County, Ohio.

213

Much further to the north-east, in Ohio, another lost race of native Americans left a remarkable structure behind them. It is called Serpent Mound, in Adams County, east-south-east of Cincinnati. The mound is a serpentine earthwork 411 m (1,348 ft) long, occupying a bluff which overlooks Bush Creek. The end of the tail is a spiral, and the head of the curvilinear form has its jaws open, cradling an egg-shaped earthwork, which archaeologists now interpret as being a front-view of the mouth of a striking snake. This remarkable feature was built either by the Adena or Hopewell people, probably around two thousand years ago. Excavations through the mound at various points revealed a careful structure but no burials or artefacts.

The site's purpose is not known, but it is clearly an important and major site. What is most telling is that it is located on an unusual geological feature, probably unique in the whole of the USA—a highly localized, compact area of intensive faulting. It is called 'cryptovolcanic', because geologists cannot determine whether it was created by a volcano or by meteoric impact. There are also said to be uranium deposits in the area. That such an exceptional monument should have been built on this unique geological site is not accidental.

Back in the Old World, again at the great complex of stones around Carnac, Brittany, Pierre Méreaux *et al.* have noted (1981) that

> the granulitic platform, of which Carnac occupies the approximate centre, is surrounded by 31 faults. Now, if we talk about faults, we are talking about the possibility of seismic activity. Quite to the contrary of what one might suppose, it is not the volcanic Auvergne that is the area with the most seismic activity in France, but the south of Morbihan. The index of average seismicity in France is 4 (annual number of tremors per 100,000 square kilometres), and that of Sud-Morbihan reaches 7.9, which is double!

PLATE 99 Looking towards the tail of the Serpent Mound, Ohio.

In Part Two we noted that the great shrine site now occupied by Bath is on a fault. This sacred spring is reminiscent in character of one of Greece's most important sanctuaries—Delphi. This sits on the slopes of Mount Parnassos, and flourished from 700 to 200 BC. Like many major sacred centres, Delphi was considered to be the navel of the world and was marked by a stone *omphalos* (now in the Delphi museum). The importance of the site, which was probably a religious centre as far back as the Bronze Age, arose because of a fissure in the ground that issued vapours. Anyone inhaling these became semi-conscious, entering a trance. The cult of Apollo superseded an earlier Ge (Gaia, Mother Earth) dedication in a temple built on the fissure. Nearby is the Castalia spring, said to have been created when the winged-horse, Pegasus, struck the ground with his hoof, and to be haunted by the three Muses.

The place was used as an oracle, and the prophetess (the *Pythia*) would take a drink of the spring water then mount a tripod seat over the fissure, going into trance due to the vapours. (Hallucinogenic laurel leaves were also burned, it seems.) Her mumblings during trance formed the basis of the oracular pronouncements, the sounds being translated by specialized interpreters as answers to questions.

The vapours seem to have risen from a water source in the fissure beneath the temple (Branigan, 1982). This source cannot be found today, but archaeologists think that 'a channel routed under the foundations could perhaps have been tapped' (*ibid.*). The site is subject to electrical storms and earthquakes.

Finally, northwards to Iceland. Here not any old fault was used, but the great rift where the North American and Eurasian tectonic plates pull apart: a northwards extension of the mid-Atlantic ridge, slicing

FIG. 30 A design from a fourth-century AD Greek vase showing King Aegeus of Athens consulting the *Pythia* on her tripod at Delphi.

215

south-west–north-east through Iceland. On this awesome geological feature, in AD 930, the main Icelandic law court, parliament, Moot site, and ceremonial centre, the *Althing* was sited at a rift valley called Thingvellir. It is now 10.5 m (35 ft) wider than when it was first used due to the remorseless tectonic stress. A major feature at this place is called Almannagja—Rift Rock of the People. It is 36.5 m (120 ft) high and 7.2 km (4.5 miles) long. Katherine Scherman has graphically described it (1976):

> Walking along it, the sense of the earth splitting apart beneath one is very strong. The rock has pulled apart jaggedly; pushed back together again the margins would fit, like pieces of a jigsaw puzzle. If it weren't for chickweed and moss campion growing in the crevices the cliff might have only just fractured.

Near the top of Almannagja is an opening, where there is a big boulder called the Law Rock. This was where the Law Speaker stood and repeated the words of the Law from memory, his voice amplified by the rift rock.

This geological feature was deliberately sought by the Scandinavian settlers, and its major nature made it appropriate as the setting for the community's key site. There is no fundamental difference between the people of the first millennium AD and the second and third millennia BC. If the Icelanders had a sense, ability, and need to site their ceremonial site on a fault, it is a practice that must have originated somewhere, perhaps back in the mists of prehistory. We know the megalith builders could read geology well. They knew where to mine flint, and where to find and quarry certain stone. The people of the Bronze Age knew how to prospect for minerals. There can be no doubt that they had the ability to perceive faulting, quite apart from the observation of the phenomena that haunted such places.

The ancient sites of power were sometimes found, and sometimes deliberately constructed to mimic or enhance what could be found in Nature. In either case, the forces of the natural world were used. And they were used for a variety of purposes, such as the promotion of fertility and for healing. But the over-riding purpose was the need to have gateways through which contact with spirit could be achieved. In the ancient world there were certain people who knew how to work with the physical world in order to create access to the spiritual.

These raw, elemental places have much to tell us about how they were used, and consequently how they can be used as tools by us today to get closer in touch with our souls and the Earth itself.

Let us hope we will have the sense to seek, the wisdom to listen, and the patience to learn.

REFERENCES

Addresses:
The Dragon Project Trust: always seeking financial, logistical and volunteer support, can be contacted in the first instance via:
Paul Devereux: Website: http://www.acemake.com/PaulDevereux

*The Ley Hunter, P.O. Box 92, Penzance, Cornwall TR18 2XL.
**UFO Brigantia, 84 Elland Road, Brighouse, West Yorkshire.

Barnatt, John (1978) *Stone Circles of the Peak*, Turnstone Press, Wellingborough.
Barnatt, John (1982) *Prehistoric Cornwall—The Ceremonial Monuments*, Turnstone Press, Wellingborough.
Becker, Robert O. (1985) *The Body Electric*, Wm Morrow, New York.
Benner, Susan (1988) 'Where ancient peoples thrived', *New York Times*, 2 October.
Bennett, Paul (1985) Personal communication documented in *UFO Brigantia***, no. 11.
Bennett, Paul (1986) 'Events in the Annals of Arran', *UFO Brigantia***, March.
Birchby, S. L. (1987) *Ten Million Rainbows*, The Newsletter Group.
Bird, Christopher (1979) *Divining*, Macdonald & Jane's.
Blofeld, John (1972) *The Wheel of Life*, Rider, London.
Bord, Janet and Bord, Colin (1976) *The Secret Country*, Elek, London.
Bord, Janet and Bord, Colin (1982) *Earth Rites*, Granada, London.
Bord, Janet and Bord, Colin (1985) *Sacred Waters*, Granada, London.
Branigan, K. (ed.) (1982) *The Atlas of Archaeology*, Macdonald, London.
Brennan, Martin (1983) *The Stars and the Stones*, Thames & Hudson, London.
Brooker, Charles (1983) 'Magnetism and the standing stones', *New Scientist*, 13 January.
Buckle, Eileen (1974) 'Welsh mountain explosion', *Flying Saucer Review Case Histories*, no. 18.
Burl, Aubrey (1976) *Stone Circles of the British Isles*, Yale University Press, New Haven, Conn.
Burl, Aubrey (1987) 'Moonwatch', *The Ley Hunter**, no. 102.

Castle, Christopher (1979) 'Megaliths in the Senegambia', *The Ley Hunter**, no. 85.
Chapman, L. (1982) 'A tingle in the fingers. . .', *The Ley Hunter**, no. 94.
Charpentier, Louis (1966) *The Mysteries of Chartres Cathedral*, Thorsons/RILKO edn, Wellingborough, 1972.
Clark, Evelyn (1961) *Cornish Fogous*, Methuen, London.
Clarke, David and Oldroyd, Granville (1985) *Spooklights—A British Survey*, private.
Congdon, Stephen (1986) 'Tor lights', *The Ley Hunter**, no. 100.
Cooke, Ian (1987) *Journey to the Stones*, Men-an-Tol Studio, Penzance.
Cooper, Roy (1980) personal comment and internal Dragon Project report dated 11 March 1980.
CNN (1987) 'Radon mines', *Newsnight*, 22 November.

Critchlow, Keith (1979) *Time Stands Still*, Gordon Fraser, London.
Cunliffe, Barry (1985) *The Roman Baths and Museum*, Bath Archaeological Trust, Bath.

Dem, Marc (1977) *Megaliths et Routes Secretes de l'Uranium*, Michel, Paris. (English translation courtesy of Christine Rhone).
Devereux, Paul (1979) 'Pipers at the Gates of Dawn', *The Ley Hunter**.
Devereux, Paul (1982) *Earth Lights*, Turnstone Press, Wellingborough.
Devereux, Paul (1989) *Earth Lights Revelation*, Blandford Press, London.
Devereux, Paul and Devereux, Jay (1980) 'The Coldrum Ley', *The Ley Hunter**, no. 88.
Devereux, Paul, McCartney, Paul, and Robins, Don (1983) 'Bringing UFOs down to earth', *New Scientist*, 1 September.
Devereux, Paul and Mullard, Jonathan (1983) 'The first Gaia', *Earthlines*, no. 1.

Edwards, Lewis (1948) 'The Welsh Temple of the Zodiac', *Research*.
Eitel, E. J. (1973) *Feng Shui*, Cokaygne, Cambridge (published in 1873 as *The Rudiments of Natural Science in China*).
Eliade, Mircea (1964) *Shamanism—Archaic Techniques of Ecstasy*, Princeton University Press Bollingen edn.
Eogan, George (1986) *Knowth*, Thames & Hudson, London.
Erde und Kosmos (1985) 'Begegnung mit steinen der Megalithkultur', April.

Fernie, William T. (1907) *The Occult and Curative Powers of Precious Stones*, Harper & Row, New York, (1973 edn.).

Gleick, James (1987) *Chaos: Making a New Science*, Viking Penguin, New York.
Glover, John A. (1980) 'Paths of light and shadow', *The Ley Hunter**, no. 87.
Graves, Tom (1986) *The Diviners Handbook*, Aquarian Press, Wellingborough, (first published 1976 as *Dowsing*, Turnstone Press, Wellingborough).
Grinsell, Leslie V. (1976) *Folklore of Prehistoric Sites in Britain*, David & Charles, Newton Abbot.
Grinsell, Leslie V. (1981) *Mitchell's Fold Stone Circle and its Folklore*, Toucan Press, Guernsey.
Guardian (1974) 'Earth tremors in the north', 24 January.

Harte, Jeremy (1986) *Cuckoo Pounds and Singing Barrows*, Dorset Natural History and Archaeology Society, Dorchester.
Hawkes, Jacquetta (1973) *A Guide to the Prehistoric and Roman Monuments in England and Wales*, Cardinal, London.
Hitching, Francis (1976) *Earth Magic*, Cassell, London.
Howells, William (1948) *The Heathens*, Doubleday, New York.

Kalweit, Holger (1988) *Dreamtime and Inner Space*, Shambhala, Boston.

Lambrick, George (1983) *The Rollright Stones*, Oxford Archaeological Unit, Oxford.
Leggat, P. O. and Leggat, D. V. (1987) *The Healing Wells—Cornish Cults and Customs*, Truran, Cornwall.

Lemesurier, Peter (1977) *The Great Pyramid Decoded*, Compton Press, Tisbury.

Leroy-Gourham, Arlette (1975) 'The flowers found with Shanidar IV, a Neanderthal burial in Iraq', *Science*, 7 November.

Lévy-Bruhl, Lucien (1935) *Primitive Mythology*, University of Queensland Press, St. Lucia, Queensland (1983 edn.).

Ley Hunter, The* (1977) no. 74, p. 20.

Lip, Evelyn (1979) *Feng Shui*, Heian, Union City edn, 1987.

Lovejoy, Alan (1988) 'Magnetic anomaly at the Long Stone', *Gloucestershire Earth Mysteries*, no. 7 (49 Moorend Rd, Leckhampton, Cheltenham, Glos. GL53 0ET).

Mac Manus, Dermot (1973) *The Middle Kingdom*, Colin Smythe, Gerrards Cross.

Magin, Ulrich (1988) 'German Earth Mysteries', *The Ley Hunter**, no. 106.

Mankowicz, Dr Paul (undated) via personal communication from Prof. Bethe Hagens.

McKenna, Terence (1988) 'Hallucinogenic mushrooms and evolution', *ReVISION*, spring.

McClure, Kevin and McClure, Sue (1980) *Stars and Rumours of Stars*, private.

Méreaux, Pierre, and the Kadath team (1981) *Carnac—une Porte vers l'Inconnu*, Laffont, (English translations courtesy of Christine Rhone).

Mertz, Blanche (1987) *Points of Cosmic Energy* (English edition), C. W. Daniel, Saffron Walden.

Michell, John (1969) *The View Over Atlantis*, Sago, London.

Michie, U. McL. and Cooper, D. C. (1979) *Uranium in the Old Red Sandstone of Orkney*, HMSO, London.

Morrison, Tony (1987) *The Mystery of the Nasca Lines*, Nonesuch Press, London.

Mountford, Charles P. (1968) *Winbaraku—and the Myth of Jarapiri*, Rigby, Adelaide.

Neihardt, John G. (1932) *Black Elk Speaks*, Pocket Books, (1972 edn.).

NRPB (1981) *Living with Radiation*.

Pennick, Nigel and Devereux, Paul (1989) *Lines on the Landscape*, Hale, London.

Pepper, Elizabeth and Wilcock, John (1977) *Magical and Mystical Sites*, BCA, Swindon.

Persinger, Michael A. (1977) *Space-Time Transients*, Nelson-Hall, (and many papers by Prof. Persinger).

Persinger, Michael A. and Schaut, G. B. (1988) 'Geomagnetic factors in subjective telepathic, precognitive and postmortem experiences', *Journal of the American Society for Psychic Research*, July.

Roberts, Anthony (1978) 'Glastonbury—The Ancient Avalon', in A. Roberts (ed.) *Glastonbury—Ancient Avalon, New Jerusalem*, Rider, London.

Robins, Don (1980) 'The Dragon awakens', *The Ley Hunter**, no. 87.

Robins, Don (1982) 'The Dragon Project and the talking stones', *New Scientist*, 21 October.

Robins, Don (1985) *Circles of Silence*, Souvenir Press, London.

Scherman, Katherine (1976) *Iceland—Daughter of Fire*, Gollanz, London.

Screeton, Paul (1974) *Quicksilver Heritage*, Thorsons, Wellingborough.

Scullard, H. H. (1979) *Roman Britain*, Thames & Hudson, London.

Shallis, Michael (1988) *The Electric Shock Book*, Souvenir Press, London.

Sharkey, John (1982) 'Mapping beyond the Minches', *The Ley Hunter**, no. 92.

Sington, T. (1919) 'A mystery', *English Mechanic and World of Science*, no. 2847, 17 October.

Skinner, Stephen (1982) *The Living Earth Manual of Feng-Shui*, Routledge & Kegan Paul, London.

Soffe, Graham and Clare, Tom (1988) 'New evidence of ritual monuments at Long Meg and Her Daughters, Cumbria', *Antiquity*, no. 62, September.

Steele, John (1982) Internal Dragon Project report. Observer's name known but withheld pending permission.

Swentzell, Rina *An Understated Sacredness*, MASS, University of New Mexico.

Tanat Chronicle (1980) autumn.

Thom, A. (1967) *Megalithic Sites in Britain*, Oxford University Press.

Times, The (1974) 'Meteorite hunt after explosion in the Mountains', 25 January.

Tributsch, Helmut (1982) *When the Snakes Awake*, MIT Press, Cambridge, Mass.

Watson, Lyall (1974) *Supernature*, Coronet, London.

West, John Anthony (1985) *The Traveller's Key to Ancient Egypt*, Knopf, New York.

Williams, W. J. and Stoddart, D. M. (1978) *Bath—Some Encounters with Science*, Kingsmead Press, Clevedon.

Williamson, Tom (1987) 'A sense of direction for dowsers?', *New Scientist*, 19 March.

Wirtz, Paul, cited in Lucien Lévy-Bruhl (1932) *Primitive Mythology op. cit.*

Woolf, Michael and Garcia, Rachel (1977) 'Sunset with the Blind Fiddler', *Meyn Mamyro*, no. 4 (51 Carn Bosavern, St Just-in-Penwith, Cornwall).

Yensen, Richard (1988) 'From mysteries to paradigms: humanity's journey from sacred plants to psychedelic drugs', *ReVISION*, spring.

Zink, David D. (1979) *The Ancient Stones Speak*, Paddington Press, London.

INDEX